T0332704

CASE TECHNOLOGY

A Special Issue of the
Journal of Systems Integration

Edited by:

Raymond T. Yeh
Syscorp International, Inc

Reprinted from the Journal of Systems Integration
Vol. 1, Nos. 3/4 (Nov. 1991)

KLUWER ACADEMIC PUBLISHERS
Boston/Dordrecht/London

Distributors for North America:
Kluwer Academic Publishers
101 Philip Drive
Assinippi Park
Norwell, Massachusetts 02061 USA

Distributors for all other countries:
Kluwer Academic Publishers Group
Distribution Centre
Post Office Box 322
3300 AH Dordrecht, THE NETHERLANDS

Library of Congress Cataloging-in-Publication Data

CASE technology / edited by Raymond T. Yeh.
     p. cm.
    "Reprinted from the Journal of systems integration, vol. 1, nos.
3/4 (Nov. 1991)".
    Includes index.
    ISBN 0-7923-9189-6
    1. Computer-aided software engineering.   I. Yeh, Raymond Tzuu
-Yau, 1937-
  QA76.758.C365   1991
  005.1--dc20   91-36554
                                              CIP

Printed on acid-free paper.

Printed in the United States of America

CONTENTS

Journal of Systems Integration, 1, 263–264 (1991)
© 1991 Kluwer Academic Publishers, Boston. Manufactured in The Netherlands.

Editorial

This issue consists of a collection of articles related to the software process and its automation. Although great expectations have been given to computer-aided software engineering (CASE) in the last few years, the potential has not yet been fully realized. This was due in part to the immaturity of the tools, but also in part to the lack of supplementary technologies to make CASE truly viable commercially. In fact, to take any substantial field of innovation to a commercial success, it usually requires the integration of several diverse component technologies. For example, from the Wright brothers' success at Kitty Hawk in 1903, it took 30 years to bring about commercial air travel. The success of the DC-3 depended on an ensemble of five critical component technologies.

In the case of software automation, powerful cost-effective desktop computer and communication fabrics are needed technologies, as well as tool integration within a CASE environment. These component technologies are mostly here. Recent attempts, such as IBM's effort to put together an integrated CASE environment called AD/Cycle, have helped to accelerate the standardization effort. What the industry has learned, among other things, is that a process needs to be in place before the deployment of tools. In his article here, Watts Humphrey articulates well, "Automation can make an effective process more effective, but it can make a chaotic process even worse—and at considerable expense."

The articles in this issue provide a sample of this field. The first, by Yeh et al., illustrates a new process model with an example. It suggests that process models need to break away from the traditional linear cause-effect mind-set and take a multidimensional system view. It suggests that a framework for process modeling needs to include not only the activity perspective of tasks and their dependencies and scheduling but also communication structure and infrastructure perspectives. The roles of stakeholders and the communication channels among them must be made explicit by building a communication structure to effectively manage a project. Finally, the long-term objectives of an organization, such as continuing quality and productivity improvements, need to be instantiated through concrete infrastructure building, such as adoption of a total quality management program or the creation of a corporate reuse policy. The most important aspect of this article is that each perspective acts both as a reinforcing and a limiting force on the other perspectives, and hence they must coevolve together. It is a holistic or systemic approach that can better help managers to make hard trade-offs among alternatives.

Humphrey relates CASE planning to software process maturity levels. Unless an organization's process is at least under statistical control, there is no point in automation. This article makes specific suggestions as to how an organization can plan for CASE from the perspective of process. Humphrey suggests the following four steps, once the decision is made to proceed with CASE planning and illustration: accessing the organization, establishing a software engineering process group, establishing a CASE support group, and planning, managing, and tracking process improvement.

The next three articles discuss a specific tool environment for requirements/specification, prototyping of parallel programs, and automatic test data generation. Johnson et al. discuss a requirements/specification environment called Acquisition of Requirements and Incremental Evolution of Specifications (ARIES). A major problem in building large systems is the inability to capture the right requirements. Yet, mistakes made at this phase are the most expensive to correct. Johnson illustrates both the difficulty and significance. ARIES is a transformation-based system in that informally stated requirements can gradually be formalized and elaborated. The system provides support for a group of analysts working together on different analysis tasks. It also uses graphical visualization of requirements or tests them against a running simulation to support their validation. ARIES' capability for describing systems from different viewpoints and assisting the analysts in reconciling these differences is very helpful. A key reason for ARIES' powerful capability is the integration of domain knowledge into the system.

Acosta discusses a CASE environment called PProto, for prototyping parallel programs. The availability of massively parallel architecture is extremely attractive for high-performance applications; however, architecting software systems to exploit the performance afforded by the parallel processors remains a difficult challenge. Utilizing graphical visualization techniques, PProto supports mechanisms for specifying scheduling, concurrency, data dependencies, synchronization, and performance characteristics of multiple processing threads.

Offutt discusses an integrated automatic test data generation system called Godzilla. Integrating mutation analysis with other testing techniques, such as statement coverage, branch coverage, domain perturbation, and symbolic execution, the Godzilla system is a fully automatic test data generator for unit test. Such a system is practically very useful in light of the aggregate amount of time spent by programmers on unit test.

Finally, Holtkamp and Weber discuss the object management machine (OMM). OMM is an integration framework for preexisting data management systems. An OMM enables the creation of uniform access patterns to different data management systems, including query interface and transaction processing. During software development, a large set of documents of different types, such as requirements, design, test reports, and user manuals, will be produced. However, as of today, these documents are most likely being produced using different tools with tool-specific data management capabilities. OMM provides a way to homogenize data management in software development environments.

This issue provides a glimpse of what future integrated CASE is likely to bring. I hope you will enjoy reading the articles.

Raymond T. Yeh
Austin, Texas

2

Journal of Systems Integration, 1, 265–282 (1991)
© 1991 Kluwer Academic Publishers, Boston. Manufactured in The Netherlands.

A Systemic Approach to Process Modeling

RAYMOND T. YEH
International Software Systems, Inc., 9430 Research Blvd., Bldg. 4, #250, Austin, TX 78759-6543

REINHARD A. SCHLEMMER, ROLAND T. MITTERMEIR
Institut f. Informatik der Universität Klagenfurt, Universitätsstraße 65–67, A-9022 Klagenfurt, Austria

"Small Is Beautiful" — Ernst Fredrich Schumacher
"Give me a lever long enough...and single-handed I can move the world" — Archimedes

(Received March 7, 1991; Revised May 14, 1991)

Abstract. This article presents a system's view of a common sense management model for systems (COSMOS) [1]. Salient features of COSMOS are introduced through the unfolding story of process development of a hypothetical corporation called IM Co. This systemic view models the dynamic complexity of a system or organization so that inerrelationships, rather than things, patterns of changes, rather than snapshots, are captured. COSMOS views changes as an ongoing opportunity and provides guidance for system changes to be performed in small steps. However, these small steps can build a long lever that is capable of producing dramatic effects. When performing changes, essential trade-offs have to be considered. COSMOS provides three perspectives—activity, communication, and infrastructure—of a process to assist managers in dealing with these trade-offs. The model also includes a generic two-level hierarchy—control and execution levels—to keep balance among the three perspectives.

Key Words:

1. Introduction

The pervasive view of software management as practiced today is geared toward delivering an initial system within a forced schedule so that after projects have been "successfully" completed, people often realize that the project did not meet the long-term objectives. Long-term product objectives include things such as application flexibility, ease of maintenance, ease of enhancement, etc. Long-term project objectives include things like providing knowledge, tools, and system components for future projects. Such objectives are critical success factors to systems evolution or the organization in which the software process is embedded. Many projects neglect these objectives because long-term objectives are not seen as a main driving force that limits system development efforts or long-term objectives are not explicitly stated and communicated.

The inability to incorporate long-term objectives in system development leads to gradual deterioration of the organization as a whole. Such failures stem from improperly handling the basic trade-off of *broad* versus *narrow-scope objectives* within system development projects. We believe that the key to successful management of systems evolution lies in reaching a balance among three essential trade-offs. In addition to the system just mentioned, the other two are stability versus flexibility and modularity versus interconnectivity.

3

Management needs to consider the *stability* versus *flexibility trade-off* to meet the need of predictability and control without losing the necessary flexibility. Flexibility is needed in order to deal with projects that are complex, ill defined, or poorly understood. However, current practices are too dependent on schedules to force stability and end up with unstable and inflexible products.

The *modularity* versus *interconnectivity trade-off* has to be considered because complex systems demand interactions among diverse stakeholders and consideration of many interrelated concerns. On the other hand, development of such complex system calls for a certain degree of modularity in order not to lose oversight. Management needs to balance carefully between these issues. It becomes even more difficult to make rational decisions among the three essential trade-offs just mentioned as the complexity of a system or its environment increases. This is particularly true of the dynamic complexity generated by the interactions of many factors, some of which are social and economical such as the ones listed as follows:

- *Beyond software:* Large-scale projects are not just software projects, they are system development projects dealing with the integration of various types of elements software, hardware, and firmware.
- *Beyond a single producer:* For any modern system of moderate size, one would buy many components and integrate into the system and only develop a portion of the system from scratch.
- *Beyond a single client:* Systems involve people. Systems development has to account for the fact that the various individuals affected by the system development effort will have different expectations with respect to the anticipated system. Moreover, the organization they are cooperating with will usually be subject to change by having the system put into operation. Therefore, regardless of whether the "organization" for which the development effort is undertaken has a monocratic decision structure or not, we have to recognize the differences in aims and perspective with various decision makers. We need to find ways of highlighting and accommodating ambiguities and contradictions among them.
- *Beyond a single project:* We should recognize the interactions between the development effort at hand and other development tasks that are executed in parallel at the customer site as well as at the various producers or suppliers. Hence, being aware of these efforts and considering them as intervening environmental factors, we can recognize opportunities of synergism as well as threats for deviations from objectives.
- *Beyond technology:* Large-scale development efforts stretch beyond a pure technical answer to problems. Projects are embedded into living organizations. Organizations are made up and run by people, having their very specific characteristics and limitations that need to be taken into account if the projects are finally to succeed. Hence, the development effort has to consider the various psychological, social, economical, and technical aspects inherent in any system embedded into living organizations.

COSMOS—a common-sense management model for systems—[1] takes into consideration these aspects of dynamic complexity. It provides three perspectives on a process by which the trade-offs can be handled more easily. In Section 2, we use an example to set the stage for introducing COSMOS in Section 3. In Section 4, we discuss how COSMOS is applied to this example.

2. An Example—A Situation Analysis of the IM Company

This section describes the basic situation of International Manufacturing Company (IM Co.), an industrial organization producing medium- to high-technology parts for integration into industrial products. Based on this hypothetical problem statement and the desired goal, we describe two unsuccessful systems development attempts. With this knowledge we then describe how COSMOS can be applied to the problems of complex systems development in Section 4.

2.1. Basic Situation

The IM Co. has had several problems. It had a backlog up to many months when it should have been only one to two weeks. Its excellent past reputation had been soured with its customers. Another problem complicating the situation, however, was an obvious decline in the product quality, causing a rise in manufacture rejects and risk of losing important customers. To compensate, IM dropped its prices and enforced additional quality control mechanisms at the end of the manufacturing process. Unfortunately, most faulty items had already been gone through a very cost-intensive process, so much effort was being wasted.

A further complication was insufficient flow of material and prefabricates around the plant. This was due to communication problems between the order processing and manufacturing groups. Data about the production process was inappropriate and untimely. After analyzing the situation and discovering these problems, the president of IM Co. stated a goal to improve on the three critical success factors: time, quality, and cost. The following high-level strategy was adopted:

- Reduce the production cycle time
- Perform parts integration technology reusing parts and production technology
- Improve the production and design process by providing adequate data for both and establishing a direct linkage between them
- Optimize the general information flow by analyzing the real information needs at each site and establishing corresponding links
- Optimize the flow of material and the corresponding information flow
- Improve product quality by improving process quality

For implementation, IM Co. chose a computer-integrated manufacturing (CIM) strategy consisting of computer-aided design (CAD), computer-aided manufacturing (CAM), computer-aided production planning (CAP), computer-aided quality assurance (CAQ), and the necessary links to the already existing order processing system and company administration.

2.2. First Try: A One-Dimensional Approach

This subsection describes IM's first attempt to solve the problem. The original problem analysis revealed subprojects and activities to achieve the desired result. The solution to the problem was seen mainly as a technical one, so a small team of technicians immediately started scheduling implementation of a new and improved manufacturing system. Top-level management and the data processing (DP) department defined the mean tasks to be performed. Based on these, DP carefully mapped out the following structure of activities:

1. Establishing a production process data base and procedures for process monitoring
2. Providing a network for information flow on the shop floor
3. Establishing an information link between design and manufacturing to transfer design data to the shop floor and process data to the engineering and drafting department
4. Automating the manufacturing process by introducing computerized process control and robotics.
5. Procuring needed equipment and components

This approach initially led to good results rapidly so that the team did not pay further attention to the process. Soon, however, the project ran into trouble because communication was inappropriate. Most of the relevant stakeholders were not included in the project team's decision-making process. And for the ones who were included the team provided inadequate communication channels. Consequently, after an initial period of "progress," communication difficulties began to hamstring the project. The team was unable to continue activities on schedule. The different stakeholders on the shop floor and in the rest of the company were unhappy both with the intended solution and the fact that they were excluded. They blocked further progress by opposing every project team decision and either rejected or improperly used parts of the installed system.

2.3. Second Try: A Two-Dimensional Approach

Emerging from the initial activity "myopia" and recognizing the influence of another process dimension, the team set out to examine the design and implementation issues of communication. Thinking explicitly about communication structure, the team was able to define their various roles, responsibilities, and interdependencies. The team implemented effective communication channels. By doing so, they gained the stability management needs to predict and control within another perspective on the process. Thus, they were able to provide more flexibility on the activity perspective without losing on the necessary stability.

However, after several months of renewed progress, the team held a critical review of the project. This review revealed that the project was veering away from the long-term project objectives of building an open system and providing expertise and successfully applied techniques to future projects dealing with the evolution of the system. The limiting factor was the lack of concrete artifacts needed to reify the long-term, intangible objectives, although accounting for the communication structure had produced a more prolonged rise in improvement. The team recognized the need for considering the trade-off between a broad scope (long-term perspective) and a narrow scope (short-term perspective) of system development efforts. Within the first two approaches, the long-term objectives had been paid only lip service. The latter objectives had received very little attention because of the struggle to meet short-term goals and because no attempts were made to define concrete means to meet them. The team had to acknowledge that the only means to account for long-term objectives was to express them as concrete artifacts of the process. These artifacts, however, did not fit into the two existing structures. Thus, the need for a third perspective arose, and the team added infrastructure as a further means in attempting to implement a CIM solution.

The three distinct views of a process—activity structure, communication structure, and infrastructure—turned out to be essential for describing, analyzing, and performing the new IM Co. process of integrated system development. They provided additional necessary handles to deal with dynamic complexity. In Section 4 we discuss how the IM team utilizes this new insight to implement a strategy based on the COSMOS process model introduced as follows.

3. An Introduction to COSMOS

In this section we briefly introduce the above developed ideas of the three process dimensions in a more formal way. For detailed treatment of this model please refer to [1]. We pointed out in the initial discussion that the challenge to software evolution management lies in reaching a balance among three essential trade-offs. Implicit in our discussion are three distinct views of what constitutes a process and the interdependence of these views.

In dealing with the flexibility versus stability trade-off, the primary concerns focus on what activities need to be done and how these activities (or tasks) are scheduled. These concerns, called the *activity structure*, form the core of traditional process models. The activity structure models the "how" of a process. The activity structure is expressed mainly by three elements: definition of tasks and work products, ordering and dependencies among them, and scheduling, projecting, and tracking of events. The activity view is concerned with start–stop criteria and input–output artifacts. Although these things are essential, they fail to objectify the negotiation, analysis, and other information that go into the decisions behind them. Rationale and other decision-making support information may be lost.

Furthermore, this unidimensional view has two obvious drawbacks: it leads to thinking in terms of the linear cause—effect chain that typifies the waterfall model [2] and it addresses primarily detail complexity but ignores the more subtle dynamic complexity. In large software projects, multiple people or organizations such as users, customers, developers, and managers come together to understand problems. It takes months to hire and train new people and years to develop the systems and nurture management talent— and all of these processes interact continually. Conventional planning, analysis, and design methods are ill equipped to deal with the dynamic complexity that characterizes system development problems. The unidimensional view of a traditional process model suggests that by following a complex set of instructions (in the form of methodology), an effective software product can be produced. Although such an approach serves for tame problems, it cannot tackle dynamic complexity caused by frequent changes and interactions. The hypothetical example of the IM Co. typifies this kind of reactive thinking as a result of a linear model.

To deal with dynamic complexity, we must go beyond linear cause and effect and address interrelationships. Only then can we handle the modularity versus interconnectivity trade-off. To aid in balancing this trade-off, we suggest adding a *communication structure* as a second dimension of process modeling. A communication structure models the communication channels among all parties (customers, developers, users, buyers, etc.) To get things done, people have to exchange information, therefore it is necessary to know who is talking to whom, who should get what information from whom, and (very importantly) what form the information is in. The communication structure includes anyone who has important influence on the resulting system and its acceptance.

Explicit modeling of communication structure results in the need for three elements: roles, interconnecting communications channels, and responsibilities and dependencies.

By modeling the different roles included in system development, we ensure that all stakeholders are part of the process. Furthermore, the information to be exchanged is another important aspect of communication structure modeling. One example of such information is the intent of a design, as well as the reasoning behind it. By making what is usually viewed as a by-product of system development more explicit and conveying it as a structure to all parties, a project is more likely to be a success. Otherwise, communication occurs in an ad hoc manner and many aspects become so implicit that they risk being lost.

Based on role maps and their artifacts, capturing the communication structure, with additional information about the channels, the actual communication structure can be analyzed according to the planned structure, answering questions such as what means are available or missing, what communciation bottlenecks need special attention, and what disconnections and redundancies are there. If the concerns and roles are sufficiently detailed and well defined, then surprising and nonobvious needs should appear during needs determination, and synergistic means to meet them should become apparent as well. But activity and communications structures alone do not completely handle dynamic complexity. Subtle processes of change may lead to drastic effects that are detected too late to avoid project risk—for example, the fielding of a system that is impractical to maintain. We need the ability to see change as a process rather than as snapshots in order to deal with the broad-scope versus narrow-scope trade-off. Such an ability is derived from *infrastructure*, which we add as the third dimension of an improved systems development process model.

Infrastructure models are needed to support the achievement of project objectives. Infrastructures are also necessary for the evolution of the process. Supporting not only communciation and performance of activities but also evolution of the process itself infrastructures serve to obtain feedback about the process and establish the implied changes. It also captures the intangible long-term objective and supports their reification into more concrete goals by providing artifacts that help to meet them.

We believe that the three-dimensional activity—communication—infrastructure (ACI) view of a process model provides the information any manager (software developer, army general, etc.) needs to manage effectively. Managers do, of course, use these views but mostly by instinct and thus only implicitly. We want to make it explicit to provide a better way to perform ongoing process observation, analysis, and improvement. Furthermore, we can use knowledge about ACI to actively design a process. We can produce additional artifacts to represent the process structure for discussion with included parties concerning what the process should be within a specific context.

Note that the three dimensions of our process model interact and coevolve. Each one acts as both a reinforcing and a limiting factor for the others. For example, in order to change an organization's process from a waterfall-like process to a Rapid Iterative Production Prototyping (RIPP) [3] approach, it is necessary first to build a basic infrastructure to support this change, such as training the RIPP process, support for reuse, and acquisition of the right tools. On the other hand, if the organization cannot finance infrastructure development, then the activity structure either cannot be changed or must be changed slowly over time. Similar interactions can be seen between the activity and communication dimensions. Thus, what we have is a process model framework of three interdependent structures of activity, communication, and infrastructure that coevolve in a mutually reinforcing and limiting progression.

As Figure 1 illustrates with its three-dimensional cone, a change on either dimension causes the other dimensions to be changed too. The limiting factors of each dimension do not allow changes on any other dimension to be too big. The figure also illustrates the fact that there exists a space within which one can move from a current state to a future state. The ideal shift would be directly from the current to the future state. However, resource limitations (e.g., money) and most people's natural resistance to big changes limit their undertaking. Thus, the shift has to be performed in smaller steps, trying to follow the "ideal line" to the future state. The cone spanned by the limiting and reinforcing factors of the ACI dimensions then provides a safety zone. Moving beyond the boundaries of this cone means that the ACI dimensions are no longer balanced. By doing so, the system is put in a state where it is not resistant to threats from outside and might easily collapse.

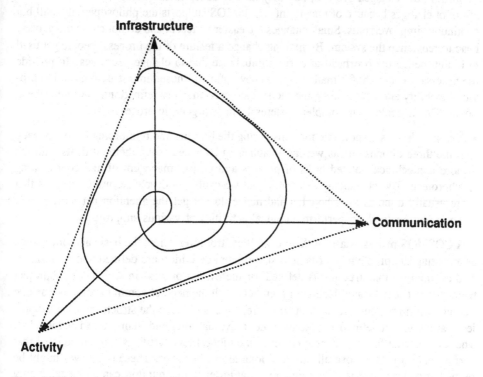

Figure 1. The coevolving framework of a process model.

So far, however, this is only a hypothesis rather than a proven fact. It is a kind of common sense that led us to these assumptions. Much work will have to be done to come up with metrics that help to identify a system's state within the ACI dimensions, to describe the desired future state, and to provide managers with means (such as metrics) to be able to see the boundaries of the cone within which they can move without causing too much unbalance and thus threaten the system.

As an example, in order to move directly from a waterfall-like process to a RIPP process, the activity structure could be changed easily to meet the RIPP activity structure. However, the waterfall model's communication structure and infrastructure are inappropriate for a RIPP activity structure. Therefore, a communication structure needs to be enhanced by new roles; new channels are opened due to the use of prototyping. This redefinition in turn causes the infrastructure to be redefined. The activity structure has to consider tasks concerned with communication (e.g., prototype demonstrations, negotiation about future directions of development effort, definition, and communication of the prototype's intent—do the users get what they see?) The infrastructure needs to be enhanced to provide rules for communication, tools for prototyping, training of project members, and users in communicating with each other, etc.

All these changes would be performed on a socioeconomic system. Therefore, these changes take time. Infrastructures cannot be built easily. Techniques and tools need to be mastered. People have to learn about the intention of changes, they have to learn now to perform in the changed process, and they have to accept these changes. Most people are afraid of changes because of uncertainty. COSMOS supports the philosophy of small but continuous improvements. Small changes are easier to accept and do not cause much overhead to rebalance the system. By making change a feature of the process, people get used to it and, hence the overhead to correct imbalance due to change decreases. To provide the necessary oversight for managing the coevolution of these three structures and to provide flexibility and adaptability, the model can be recursively refined into multiple levels. So COSMOS deals with complex systems from two generic process levels:

- A *control level* is responsible for considering the limiting and reinforcing factors of each of the three dimensions as well as establishing balance among them. It deals with the more nontechnical related tasks of process and project management and coordinating subprojects. By introducing a control level we explicitly devote resources to tasks that are usually done as afterthoughts and hence do not get the attention needed.
- An *execution level*, to perform technical activities of various subprojects.

A COSMOS process starts with an overall control level where the basic activities, such as assessing the problem, merits, and subproblem definition are defined and performed. The communication structure is defined for the overall process in which the subproject teams are not seen as a collection of members with the need of communcation but as one "point" within the communication structure. This is because the structure of the subproject team is not yet defined and therefore no individual roles and channels can be modeled. The same is true for the infrastructure; at the highest level artifacts can be modeled that correspond only to the overall projects' long-term objectives. These objectives might be refined or additional objectives might occur at lower levels, but they can be modeled only at the level where they occur.

The subprocesses are defined dynamically during performance of the overall process, which assesses the problem and decomposes it into subproblems. If control is handed over to a subproblem and it turns out to be tame enough, the process for solving it can be defined immediately by describing the necessary technical activities to be performed within the overall structure (execution level). Otherwise a control level is introduced again, performing the same task as the overall control level process, except that it is done for the smaller subproblem. The scope of this control-level process is smaller than the scope of the higher control-level process. Of course, the decomposition can be applied recursively to the subprocess. A benefit of this approach is that we do not define the process more than we really can based on the information we have at a certain time. Therefore we avoid constructing processes that are not appropriate to the problem and context in which it is to be solved. The process grows with the knowledge we gain about the problem. *The process needs to coevolve with the problem definition.*

To provide an effective linkage among subsequent control and execution levels we illustrate here a structure proposed by [4], which builds on the linking-pin structure of Likert [5]. The idea is to have one member of each subproject team as a linkage to the higher level by including him in the higher-level team. Also, horizontal linkages between subprojects can be established such that these subprojects "share" a member. Thus, we also can provide necessary coordination between subprojects working together very closely. A sketch of such a linking-pin structure is given in Figure 2.

4. How IM Co. Applied the Ideas of COSMOS

The IM Co. project team decided to redefine the process and begin again, using the ideas gained from the project problem analysis and the COSMOS model. The next sections give a high-level description of how the new process covered the ACI dimensions. For the purpose of this example we show a diagram of the process after it has already gone through a continuous cycle of improvements.

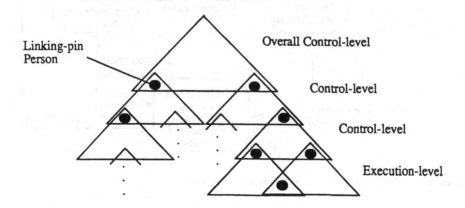

Figure 2. Linking-pins within the process hierarchy.

4.1. Two Levels of Activity Structure

We present a control level and an execution level of the activity structure for this example.

The IM Company's managerial tasks to be performed at the control level were concerned mainly with defining subprojects and providing the necessary coordination for them. These tasks were to:

1. Define long-term project objectives.
2. Perform preproject evaluation based on these objectives.
3. Device a solution strategy by defining necessary execution-level subprojects for CAD, CAM, CAP, and CAQ.
4. Establish infrastructure to meet project needs and those of subprojects, if known.
5. Establish communication structure, monitoring its adequacy and effectiveness, and adapting it when necessary.
6. Schedule and coordinate execution-level projects, accepting and assessing their results.
7. Integrate of (intermediate) results obtained from the execution levels.
8. Repeat steps 4 to 7, paying attention to process improvement.

The activity structure for these tasks is shown in Figure 3.

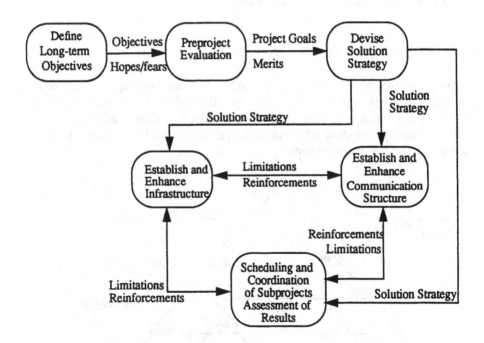

Figure 3. Part of the activity structure at the overall control level.

The structure was further refined at the execution level. Here are just a few of the tasks from the CAM subproject:

1. Design optimal production flow at the shop floor.
2. Derive optimal information flow from the production flow.
3. Specify machines needed.
4. Assess vendors and decide which ones to buy.
5. Design and implement interfaces between different machines.
6. Design the detailed information flow and necessary procedures based on network parameters and the different machine interfaces.

The activity structure for these tasks is shown in Figure 4.

4.2. Two Levels of Communciation Structure

The communication structure evolved over time, as did the other two dimensions. At the overall control level the project team established the following communication structure. The primary roles at this level were:

- *Top-level managers:* Responsible for initiating a corporate objectives analysis, formulating the primary problem statement, negotiating and deciding budget and schedule, providing users for further requirements, and signing off on the system.

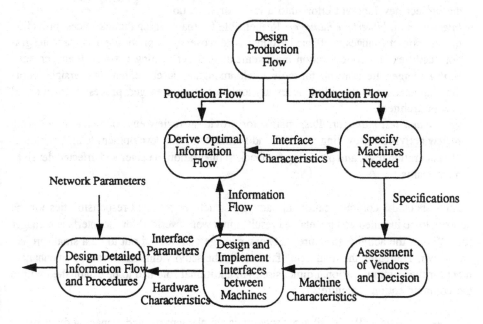

Figure 4. Parts of the activity structure at an execution level.

- *System architect:* Responsible for obtaining initial requirements from users and the primary problem statement; developing the overall system architecture; establishing the development teams; specifying subproblems, objectives, budgets; and schedules for the teams; specifying the primary interfaces between subgroups; establishing the process and providing process data for the process manager; monitoring the development efforts; and balancing the ACI structures with system oversight.
- *Project manager:* Responsible for overall project management, problem oversight, negotiating schedules and budgets with top management, providing additional resources for infrastructure, and supporting teams in managerial matters.
- *Diverse users:* Responsible for providing requirements information, system component sign-off, providing feedback about suggested solutions, and providing domain knowledge.

The group of users can be further divided into users at diverse levels within the IM Co. Sporadic users or people indirectly affected by the system ought to be included as well.

- *Process manager:* Responsible for providing a process skeleton for follow-on projects, monitoring and evolving processes, and giving feedback and feedforward concerning the process to projects.
- *Subproject teams:* Responsible for solution of the subproblems CAM, CAP, CAD, and CAQ; performing reuse (as far as is possible) and heavy user inclusion; and providing necessary interface changes to the interface manager.
- *Reuse manager:* Responsible for providing units of reuse (knowledge, requirements, design plus rationale, code, test data, and scenarios) to the development teams, the system architect, and the review and test manager to follow-on projects; incorporating results from the project development effort into a reuse organization.
- *Integration and interface manager:* Responsible for maintaining the interfaces, providing information of changes to affected groups; system oversight, providing necessary integration facilities and configuration management; and performing network management.
- *Tools manager:* Responsible for tools development and purchase, having oversight, coordinating needs, and providing necessary tools for reuse manager, process manager, and system architect.
- *Review and test manager:* Responsible for providing review environments, monitoring review activities, providing test data and scenarios to the development teams, performing integration tests, and providing feedback to integration manager and affected development teams.

Analysis of the communication and activity structures revealed responsibilities for the network to be installed and maintained resulted in a work overload for the interface manager role. Within the activity structure, network management turned out to be a small project on its own. Therefore, the reinforcing factor from the activity dimension caused an enhancement for the communicational dimension. An additional role had to be established within the communication structure:

- *Network manager:* Responsible for specifying, implementing, and managing the network needed for the implementation of the CIM strategy.

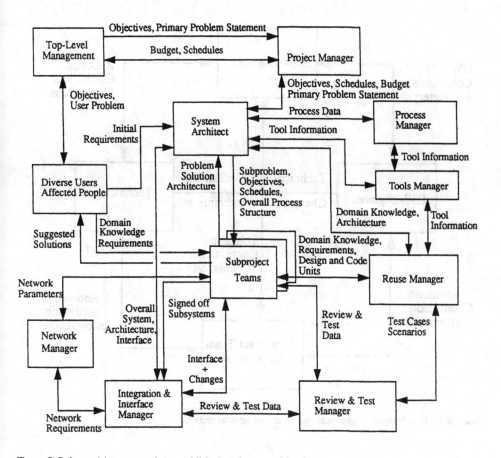

Figure 5. Roles and interconnections established at the control level.

Figure 5 shows the different roles and their interconnections. The structure was further refined at the execution level. Again, we will not elaborate on the whole communication structure but simply illustrate the refinement of the overall communication structure by looking at one subproject team. This team was responsible for the CAM part within the overall CIM strategy. The additional roles at this level were that of:

- *Software engineer(s):* Responsible for the software parts of the CAM system, defining and implementing interfaces, and specifying and selecting appropriate software within CAM.
- *Hardware engineer(s):* Responsible for specification and selection of shop–floor hardware, which includes both computer and noncomputer parts; specifying custom-made additional appliances.
- *Technicians:* Responsible for performing necessary technical changes to existing appliances, installing new machines and appliances.
- *Subproject team coordinator:* Responsible for the coordination of the other roles tasks and responsibilities as well as serving as a linking pin to the upper control level.

The interconnections for these roles are illustrated in Figure 6.

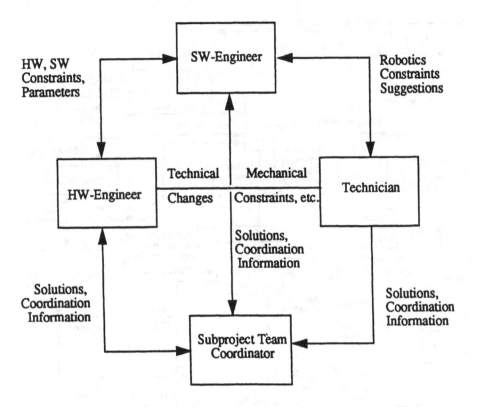

Figure 6. CAM subproject communicational roles and interconnections.

4.3. Infrastructure Established at the Control Level

The infrastructure was, like the other two dimensions, evolving over time. Thus, for our purpose we present it as a snapshot in four parts:

1. *Organization:* Organizational structures for allocating responsibilities for ongoing evaluation, testing, archiving and information management, and other tasks (i.e., mapping of communication roles and persons); well-stated and documented project objectives; personnel assessment for training of current personnel, including a training plan; proper process description, including activity and communication structure and infrastructure definitions; resources devoted to process management; resources allocated to communication, negotiation, and evaluation of activities by participants; and training material for new personnel on the process design as well as system design.
2. *Tools and technology:* Development of languages and tools; testing tools; debugging; an in-house developed configuration management tool called CONF; a process-monitoring tool; an in-house developed reuse database for code, design, and requirements; test cases and scenarios; a database of specifications of project objectives and priorities, project, and process designs (plans, organizational structure contracts, communication mechanisms, information management and access mechanisms, evaluation mechanisms);

specifications of system requirements for current and future system versions; and designs of system versions (refinements and reformulations of requirements specifications structured in terms of the system and its justification, along with programs at different levels of abstraction).

3. *Software engineering methods:* Standards for programming, testing, documenting; review mechanisms for design coding; testing; and the process itself; metrics for process monitoring and data management.

4. *Acquisition:* Acquisition method, procedure, and metrics for both hardware and software. The establishment of these artifacts reinforced a change at the activity dimension taking into consideration the procedures defined.

The introduction of the network manager into the communication structure brought about a reevaluation of the infrastructure, resulting in the addition of infrastructure elements (e.g., a network performance diagnostics tool and a network administration database).

By making the ACI dimensions explicit and considering their coevolutionary nature and by using COSMOS's two-level approach, the IM Co.'s new process for developing and implementing a CIM strategy showed steady progress. In acknowledging all three dimensions of the process, the project team was able to balance it by heeding the reinforcing and limiting forces of the ACI interdependencies.

4.4. A Hypothetical Postmortem

The three tries of the IM Co. to improve its system can be illustrated by looking at the spirallike coevolving ACI dimensions first introduced in Section 3. Figure 7 shows the original and the desired state in an abstract form.

The first try of the IM Co. was focused mostly on activities. Communication and infrastructure were not explicitly taken into consideration and thus was not planned. Therefore, this attempt can be characterized as moving only along the activity axis within our three

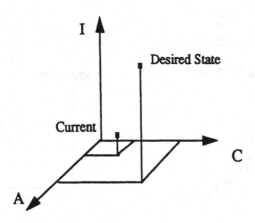

Figure 7. Original and desired state within the ACI-dimensions.

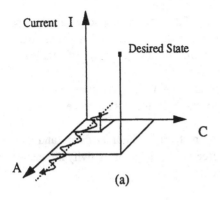

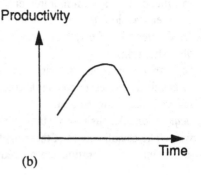

Figure 8. Looking at the activity axis only.

dimensions, as depicted in Figure 8. At the beginning, this approach reduces the distance to the desired state rapidly (as shown in Figure 8b). However, limitations caused by the neglection of communicational as well as the infrastructural dimensions (as described in Section 2) soon start to distract most of the effort spent in the process. Thus, the process spirals around the activity axis, and it becomes increasingly more difficult to get things done after some point until the process collapses eventually.

The IM Co.'s second try was characterized by neglect of the infrastructure necessary to head toward the long-term objectives while struggling with short-term problems. Figure 9 pinpoints the move of the process from the original state. There is some initial reduction of the distance between current and desired state. But since the process moves on the activity and communication axis only, by not explicitly taking into consideration the necessary third dimensions, viewed from the long-term perspective, the distance starts to increase again. If the process continues to move only within those two dimensions, it will soon collapse (as shown in Figure 9b) due to too much effort spent on struggling with problems resulting from neglection of infrastructure as a limiting factor within a process after some point.

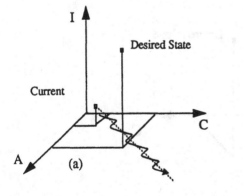

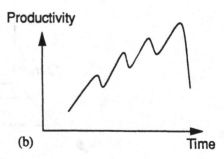

Figure 9. Looking at the activity and communication axes.

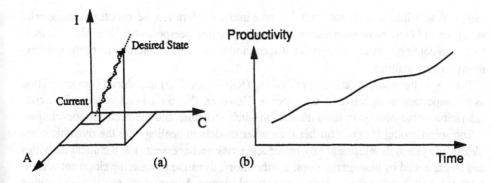

Figure 10. Considering all ACI axes.

By applying COSMOS, and thus explicitly looking at all three dimensions and their reinforcing and limiting influences on each other, the IM Co. was finally moving on all three axes from the original state to the desired state of the system. As Figure 10 indicates, there is not as much initial progress as with the other attempts because some overhead is spent on establishing the three structures and balancing them. However, using this approach one can be sure that effort spent on the process leads to the desired state and is not distracted. Figure 10b hypothesizes that COSMOS provides guidance for making steady progress. The dips in the figure are caused by the need for additional support in communication or infrastructure as well as the resulting rebalance of the process. Once established, the process can increase progress for a while until newly occurring limitations on either dimension call for some effort to be spent on rebalancing of the ACI structures. This example shows that the applicability of the COSMOS model is not limited to software systems only. It is a general management model that explicitly provides a stabilizing force among competing forces and provides guidance to make steps of continual improvements towards a goal.

5. Concluding Remarks

The evolution of process models tells the story of different attempts to manage the dynamic complexity in systems building. The ad-hoc approach was of little help in dealing with the three essential trade-offs of systems building. The waterfall model [2] tackles the problem by using a linear sequence of activities: requirements analysis, design, implementation, testing, and so forth. This linear and unidimensional perspective is not able to reach a balance among the three trade-offs and the resulting processes are too inflexible to adapt themselves to changing needs and to deal with the complexity inherent in large systems. It also turned out to be oriented too much toward a single project, thus not having the necessary long-term perspective to deal with the evolution of systems and the process itself.

Other models, like the evolutionary model [6] or the incremental model [7] introduced a more long-term-oriented view on the process, thus meeting the needs for balancing the trade-off between broad and narrow scope. Unlike the waterfall, these models are built on the premise that good solutions are hardly found in a one-shot approach and that needs change and arise during system usage. However, they are still mainly concerned with technical activities and do not explicitly take into consideration the necessary managerial activities and communicational as well as infrastructural perspectives. Thus, they are ineffective in dealing with the trade-offs between modularity versus interconnectivity and flexibility versus stability.

The Rapid Iterative Production Prototyping (RIPP) model [3] introduced communication as an important perspective of the process. However, this model lacks the explicit consideration of the necessary third dimension—infrastructure and the need for coevolution.

The spiral model [8] goes further than other models in dealing with the dynamic complexity of system development. By introducing risk management, the technical activities can be enhanced by managerial ones. Furthermore, dynamic process development was introduced, which called for certain infrastructural support. However, the spiral model neither considers these perspectives explicitly, nor the need for coevolving development of these three structures. Therefore, it still does not have the necessary integrated view for dealing with the dynamic complexity of system building.

COSMOS builds on the experience made with these approaches and uses a coevolving, three-dimensional perspective to aid managers in handling the three trade-offs. Thus, it provides a systems view on process modeling. As such, it provides guidance for managers to tackle very large projects with a multiple, contingent approach utilizing a series of small and related steps. These steps, however small, can be thought of as the basic components of a long lever, which—as Archimedes pointed out long ago—can produce dramatic effects. Of course, much work is needed to make COSMOS a practical tool for managers. Metrics and means have to be found to define the state of a system within the framework, to project a future state, and to highlight the boundaries of possible moves spanned by the limiting and reinforcing factors of the three dimensions on one another. Thus, managers will have a more practical guide on how to perform when dealing with changes to their systems.

References

1. R.T. Yeh, D. Naumann, R.T. Mittermeir, R.A. Schlemmer, G. Sumrall, J. LeBaron. "COSMOS: A commonsense management model for system." To appear in *IEEE Software Special Issue.*
2. W.W. Royce, "Managing the development of large software systems" in *Proc. IEEE WESCON.* August 1970.
3. S. Schultz, *Rapid Iterative Prototyping Guide.* DuPont Information Engineering Associates, Wilmington, DE, 1989.
4. R. Thomsett, "Managing superlarge projects: A contingency approach." *American Programmer.* vol 4, no. 6, 1991.
5. R. Likert, "The principle of supportive relationships," in *Organisation Theory.* D.S. Pugh (ed.). Penguin Books: Middlesex, 1971.
6. D.D. McCracken and M.A. Jackson, "Life cycle concept considered harmful," *ACM Software Engineering Notes.* vol. 7, no. 4, April 1982.
7. C. Floyd, "Outline of a paradigm change in software engineering," *ACM SIGSOFT Software Engineering Notes,* vol. 13, no. 2, 1987.
8. B.W. Boehm, "A spiral model of software development and enhancement," *IEEE Comput.* vol. 21, no. 5, May 1988.

Journal of Systems Integration, 1, 283–320 (1991)
© 1991 Kluwer Academic Publishers, Boston. Manufactured in The Netherlands.

Integrating Domain Knowledge, Requirements, and Specifications

W. LEWIS JOHNSON AND MARTIN S. FEATHER
USC/Information Sciences Institute, Marina del Rey, CA 90292-6695

DAVID R. HARRIS
Lockheed Sanders Signal Processing Center of Technology, Nashua, NH 03061-2034

(Received February 29, 1990; Revised February 20, 1991)

Abstract. This paper describes efforts to develop a transformation-based software environment that supports the acquisition and validation of software requirements specifications. These requirements may be stated informally at first, and then gradually formalized and elaborated. Support is provided for groups of requirements analysts working together, focusing on different analysis tasks and areas of concern. The environment assists in the validation of formalized requirements by translating them into natural language and graphical diagrams and testing them against a running simulation of the system to be built. Requirements defined in terms of domain concepts are transformed into constraints on system components. The advantages of this approach are that specifications can be traced back to requirements and domain concepts, which in turn have been precisely defined.

Key Words: Requirements analysis, knowledge-based software engineering, transformations, software reuse, software specification, software presentation.

1. Introduction

We are building a requirements/specification environment called ARIES[1] which requirements analysts may use in evaluating system requirements and codifying them in formal specifications. We are creating this environment to help us address several roadblocks in providing knowledge-based automated assistance to the process of developing formal specifications. One of the principal roadblocks is that formal specification languages are difficult to use in requirements acquisition, particularly by people who are not experts in logic. ARIES provides tools for the gradual evolution of acquired requirements, expressed in hypertext and graphical diagrams into formal specifications. The analysts invoke transformations to carry out this evolution; in general, support for rapid and coordinated evolution of requirements is a major concern. ARIES is particularly concerned with problems that arise in the development of specifications of large systems. Specification reuse is a major concern, so that large specifications do not have to be written from scratch. Mechanisms are provided for dealing with conflicts in requirements, especially those arising when groups of analysts work together. Validation techniques, including simulation, deduction, and abstraction, are provided to cope with the problem that large specifications are difficult to understand and reason about.

ARIES is an intensively knowledge-based system. It incorporates knowledge about application domains, system components, and design processes and supports analysts in applying this knowledge to the requirements analysis process.

This paper describes the ARIES system. It also describes some studies of requirements analysis activities that were used to motivate and evaluate ARIES. The purpose of these studies were twofold. First, they helped to identify needs that conventional requirements analysis tools do not meet very well, but for which knowledge-based tools could offer help. Second, they demonstrate ARIES' ability to support realistic requirements analysis tasks. In this way ARIES is shown to be not just research prototype, but a plausible model for how to build knowledge-based tools that can handle large-scale software engineering problems.

2. Background

ARIES is a product of the ongoing Knowledge-Based Software Assistant (KBSA) program. KBSA, as proposed in the 1983 report by the U.S. Air Force's Rome Laboratories [15], was conceived as an integrated knowledge-based system to support all aspects of the software life cycle. Such an assistant would support specification-based software development: programs would not be written in conventional programming languages, but instead would be written in an executable specification language, from which efficient implementations would be mechanically derived. Figure 1 shows how the authors of the report envisioned that the software would be developed in the KBSA paradigm.[2] First, the process of requirements analysis generates a formal specification from informal requirements. The formal specification is then input to a mechanical transformation process, yielding an optimized program. Validation is performed through examination and analysis of the formal specification, not by testing the optimized code. Maintenance is performed by modifying the specification, and deriving a new optimized program. In a complete KBSA system, and to some extent in ARIES as well, requirements analysis tools and implementation tools are integrated into a single environment, allowing analysts to perform exploratory prototyping during requirements analysis. Nevertheless, the design of ARIES does not preclude its use in situations where a full KBSA system is not available.

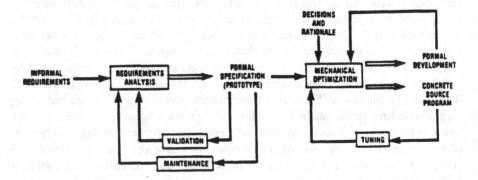

Figure 1. The original KBSA software paradigm.

The ARIES effort builds on the results of earlier efforts at USC/ISI and Lockheed Sanders. Requirements analysis was addressed in Lockheed Sanders's Knowledge-Based Requirements Assistant (KBRA) [19]. ISI developed the Knowledge-Based Assistant (KBSA) [23, 24, 31] to support specification construction, validation, and evolution.

KBRA provided facilities for acquisition of informal requirements, entered as structured text and diagrams. It had a limited case-frame-based ability to assist in the formalization of informal text by recognizing words in a lexicon of domain concepts. It allowed users to describe systems from different points of view, e.g., data flow and functional decomposition. KBRA maintained an internal representation of the system being built that integrates these different views, as do certain other CASE tools such as STATEMATE [18]. KBRA was able to generate DoD-STD-2167A-style requirements documents from its system descriptions.

The principal contribution of KBSA was the development of evolution transformations for specification modification [25]. KBSA also provided validation tools in the form of a paraphraser, which translates specifications into English [29, 38], a symbolic evaluator for simulating the specification and proving theorems about it [9], and static analysis tools which automatically maintain and update analysis information as the specification is transformed [26].

2.1. The Specification Development Process

ARIES assumes a model of software development in which there are multiple goals for requirements analysis. First, it should produce a software requirements specification (SRS), describing the characteristics of the system to be built. However, such documents are themselves but a means to achieve a more fundamental goal, i.e., communication of requirements to designers and stakeholders (endusers, procurement agents, etc.). Other communication media besides conventional text documents, such as diagrams, are also useful to accomplish successful communication. Executable prototypes are another useful product, both to help communicate requirements and to validate the accuracy of those requirements. Finally, we assume that system requirements are not developed from scratch and thrown away. Instead, a goal of the requirements analysis process should be to develop generic requirements descriptions applicable to many possible systems in the application domain and reuse such descriptions where they exist.

We make no attempt to separate requirements analysis activities from "specification" activities. This view is shared with many workers in the field of requirements analysis, such as Davis [11], within the context of conventional software development paradigms. It is also consistent with the KBSA paradigm, although KBSA affords some freedoms that conventional software development paradigms lack.

Figure 2 shows a diagram depicting in simplest terms the specification development process as supported by ARIES. An acquisition process incorporates new information about a system from analysts who may collect this information from a variety of sources, including interviews with clients and source documents describing the domain in which the system will operate. An evolution process, directed by analysts, reformulates statements about a system so that they are more precise, formal, and/or implementable. It also corrects

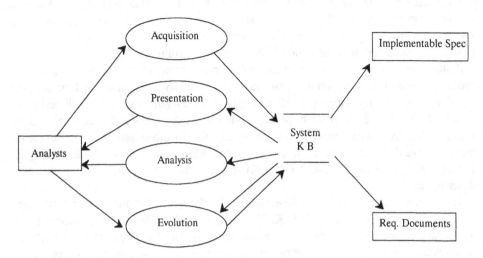

Figure 2. ARIES view of specification development.

inaccuracies in requirements and revises requirements that cannot be satisfied strictly as stated. An analysis process explores consequences of requirements statements, looking for inconsistencies.

The central focus of work in this view is the system knowledge base, a repository of knowledge about stereotypical domains, reusable requirements/specification components, and descriptions of specific systems being developed. Instead of being constructed in isolation, formal specifications are defined in terms of this knowledge base and are part of the knowledge base.

The output from this process consists of two parts: an implementable specification, which in a KBSA setting serves as input to a mechanical optimization process, and requirements communication vehicles—documents and diagrams—which describe the system to be built in precise terms. These two outputs subsume the role of SRSs in conventional software development.

2.2. *A Good Requirements Specification*

It is important to carefully describe the nature of a good requirements work product. A good software requirements specification must itself meet a number of conflicting requirements simultaneously. This makes comprehensive mechanical support for requirements analysis difficult to achieve. Davis, in his book *Software Requirments Analysis and Specification* [11], identifies several properties that an SRS should be:

- *Correct*—the requirements that it contains are in fact required of the system to be built.
- *Unambiguous*, so that each requirement may be interpreted in only way.
- *Complete*, describing all properties that the system should have.
- *Verifiable*—there is some cost-effective means for testing whether the requirement is met.

- *Consistent*—no subset of the requirements conflict.
- *Understandable by noncomputer specialists.*
- *Modifiable*—necessary changes to requirements may be made easily, completely, and consistently.
- *Traceable*—each requirement may be traced to its origin in other documents and may be traced to the software component(s) satisfying the requirement.
- *Annotated*—each requirement should be marked to indicate how necessary and volatile it is.

These properties are clearly difficult to attain at the same time. Nevertheless, it is useful to think of requirements analysis as attempting to gradually achieve them to the greatest extent possible. ARIES is designed to support the gradual establishment of these properties.

3. ARIES' Contribution

ARIES contains tools for *acquisition*, *review*, *analysis*, and *evolution*. Acquisition facilities allow analysts to build up system descriptions gradually. Review and analysis tools allow analysts to check for consistency, correctness, and ambiguity, and gauge completeness; they also help make systems descriptions understandable by noncomputer specialists. Evolution tools support modification, tracing, and evolution of requirements descriptions.

3.1. Acquisition Tools

The acquisition tools in ARIES aim to capture initial statements of requirements as simply and directly as possible. If requirements cannot be initially stated in a manner that is intuitive for the analyst or enduser, it is difficult to ensure that the requirements are correct. Acquisition in ARIES is accomplished by the following means. First, a structured text facility is employed for managing textual information found in relevant documents or in informal engineering notes. To the extent that such documents already exist and can be linked to subsequent formal specifications, ARIES can make a strong contribution to the correctness and traceability of the completed specification. Second, since natural language by itself is often awkward and ambiguous as a medium for stating requirements, other notations familiar to analysts are likewise supported: state transition diagrams, information flow diagrams, taxonomies, decomposition hierarchies, as well as formal specification languages. Third, we are experimenting with domain-specific notations, to make it possible for noncomputer specialists to describe requirements. Importantly, these notations are all mapped onto a common representation of specifications internal to ARIES.

3.2. Review

The review process in ARIES applies many of the same tools as acquisition but in reverse. Information entered into the system in one notation may be presented in a different notation.

If the analyst has the opportunity to switch point of view, correctness, and completeness of specifications can be more easily achieved. Most review tools have an analogue in the acquisition side. In fact, the internal presentaton architecture (described below) exploits such analogies whenever possible. However, there are limitations—for example, ARIES is able to translate from its formal internal descriptions to English, but it cannot translate English into formal requirements statements.

3.3. Evolution

Evolution mechanisms are central to requirements analysis in ARIES: requirements statements are expected to evolve gradually over time. *Evolution transformations* are the principal mechanism for evolution in ARIES. They are operators that modify system descriptions in a controlled fashion, affecting some aspects of a requirements statement while retaining others unchanged. They also propagate changes throughout a system description. Significant effort has been invested in ARIES in identifying evolution steps (both meaning-preserving and non-meaning-preserving) that routinely occur in the specification development process and automating them in the form of evolution transformations.

3.4. Analysis

Analysis capabilities help analysts check for inconsistencies in proposed requirements and explore consequences. Three basic types of analysis capabilities are provided. First, a simulation facility translates descriptions of required behavior into executable simulations. By running the simulations, an analyst can determine whether the stated requirements really guarantee satisfactory behavior. Deduction mechanisms propagate information through the system description, both to complete it and to detect conflicts and inconsistencies. Abstraction mechanisms employ evolution transformations to extract simplified views of the system description. These abstracted views are typically easier to validate, either through simulation or by inspection.

3.5. Reuse Tools

Requirements may be defined by specializing and adapting existing requirements in ARIES' knowledge base of common requirements; this makes it easier to define requirements quickly and accurately. *Folders* are used in ARIES to capture, separate, and relate bodies of requirements information. The analysts can control the extent to which folders share information, and gradually increase the sharing as inconsistencies are reconciled. ARIES places a heavy emphasis on codification and use of domain knowledge in requirements analysis. Although a number of researchers have identified domain modeling as a key concern (e.g., Borgida, Greenspan, and Mylopoulos [7]), it is given short shrift in typical practice. Requirements analysis is usually narrowly focused on describing the requirements for a single system. This is problematic if an organization is interested in introducing more than one computer system into an environment or when the degree of computerization of an organization is expected to increase over time. We have been modeling particular domains within ARIES, and experimenting with using such knowledge in the engineering of requirements for multiple systems.

4. Example Problems

This section describes some of our experience in using specific application domains to hone the above-mentioned tools. Although our approach to requirements analysis aims to broadly support requirements acquisition and analysis, we have concentrated on several relatively focused domains, including hospital patient monitoring, library systems, signal processing, and tracking. To demonstrate the power of the ARIES approach, and its ability to handle large complex specification problems, we have devoted significant effort to a single domain, i.e., air traffic control. We have used two sources for this work. First, we have been modeling requirements for a particular system—the control system used for air traffic control in the airspace around Tempelhof Airport in Berlin. Second, we have studied the requirements for U.S. domestic, en route air traffic control systems, i.e., those systems responsible for the control of air traffic cruising at high altitudes reserved for jets. These requirements are drawn from manuals on flight procedures (e.g., [2]) and from the experiences of the Federal Aviation Administration's Advanced Automation Program [21], whose goal is to develop the next generation of air traffic control systems. We have also interviewed requirements analysts in this domain and information processing specialists with the current air traffic control automation system.

Our investigaton has proceeded in three phases. First, under the KBRA effort, we conducted extensive interviews with air traffic control system engineers. An engineer's notebook was created, the KBSA community adopted air traffic control as a common application domain, and this domain was used to drive the development of the precursor KBRA and KBSA prototypes. Second, in the spring of 1990 ARIES project members performed an experimental exercise in the road traffic control domain. We felt that this domain would be small enough that it would be possible to analyze from beginning to end in a limited amount of time. This study provided insights into how knowledge-based tools could be employed to coordinate groups of requirements analysts. It also suggested ways of organizing domain and requirements knowledge in a reusable manner so that the same knowledge base components could be used both for air traffic control and road traffic control. Finally, we have returned to the air traffic control domain to flesh out earlier efforts based on many of the insights derived from the smaller road traffic control study.

The air traffic control experiment is still underway, as the specification of the Advanced Automation System (AAS) is expanded. At this point in time, the ARIES knowledge base consists of the following: 978 definitions of a reusable nature, 162 definitions specific to the road traffic control specification, and 353 definitions specific to the AAS specification. Our future work will expand on the AAS specification and generalize concepts in this specification so as to expand the library of reusable definitions.

The following two sections draw from these experiments. First, we describe some of the general issues that are associated with road traffic control specification; then we give a detailed analysis of a specific specification evolution in the broader air traffic control domain.

4.1. Developing a Road Traffic Control Specification

In the road traffic control exercise, each project member worked independently on one aspect of the road traffic control problem. We then compared notes to find common themes and to compare this work with the body of air traffic control requirements knowledge that we had already formalized. The following are some of the issues that different project members investigated in analyzing the road traffic control problem:

- Understanding what restrictions must be placed on the duration of traffic light signals to ensure safe and expeditious flow of traffic
- Identifying requirements by viewing the problem as an instance of a generic scheduling problem, and determining what general requirements of scheduling problems apply to road traffic control
- Identifying possible states of the traffic lights, and conditions under which the system changes state
- Sketching possible algorithms for coordinating lights

There were other issues that were not explicitly raised but that were implicit in a number of these investigations, such as how the traffic lights, the traffic light controller, and traffic sensors would be connected to each other.

One place where the tension between coordinated work and independent work was strong was in modeling the application domain. It was readily apparent that everyone had a similar intuitive model of the road traffic control domain. This included concepts such as vehicles, roads, colors, and directions. There were also common notions of system components, including traffic lights and roadbed sensors. At the same time, there were key differences in domain models, depending on what task each analyst was performing. For example, two distinct models of vehicle motion arose. In one, vehicles appear at the entrance to the intersection, traverse the intersection, and then disappear. This corresponds roughly to the information that a traffic light system has about the environment solely on the basis of what road sensors can provide. In another model, vehicles have a distance from the intersection, a velocity, and an acceleration, and approach and depart from the intersection in a continuous process. This latter model was needed to understand the requirements imposed on a traffic light system because of vehicle behavior (e.g., how much time must be allowed between light changes). We needed a way to support such conflicting models and at the same time understand how requirements stated in terms of one model might be reformulated in terms of another model.

The road traffic control analysis used several notations. No one notation would have been adequate by itself. The primary notations used were natural language, state transition diagrams, entity-relationship-attribute notations, and mathematical constraints. People would sometimes describe requirements first in natural language and then write formal statements to capture the meaning of the natural language. In order for other people to understand these formal statements, traces back to the original natural language were extremely important.

Simulation and execution were useful for getting the requirements right. Requirements statements that seemed reasonable at first in fact allowed for anomalous behavior, such as traffic lights changing unnecessarily. Simulation made it possible to understand the dynamics of the domain properly; for example, a simulation of traffic flow through the intersection helped to determine how long it takes for traffic waiting at an intersection to resume normal flow.

4.2. A Detailed Specification Scenario

We have been developing ARIES with the aim of facilitating the kinds of specification development activities described above. A complete example of such a development would be quite lengthy, since it would show specification development from different points of view and show how these views are integrated. In this section, we present a particular thread of specification development, taken from the air traffic control domain. This example highlights the use of evolution transformations in specification development. Other capabilities will be illustrated throughout the paper.

Figure 3 shows an initial view of aircraft course monitoring depicted here in a *context diagram*, a diagram showing the interactions between a system and its external environment and the information that flows between them. In these diagrams, ovals denote processes, boxes and miscellaneous icons denote objects, and double circles indicate system boundaries.

The diagram distills course monitoring to its essential elements: the interaction between aircraft and the air traffic control system (ATC). This abstracted view of the air traffic control system is useful as a basis for stating course-monitoring requirements. It is a natural abstraction for the domain, corresponding to the way flight procedures are commonly described in fliers' flight manuals [2]. We will not go into the specific details here of how far expected location and actual location are permitted to differ. Our concern is rather to ensure that course monitoring requirements stated from the fliers' point of view can be transformed into specifications of system functionality so that they can be integrated into the requirements specification. The transformed requirements should take into account the actual data interfaces of the proposed system.

Figure 4 shows a more detailed view of the air traffic control process. In this view, more of the agents of the proposed system are introduced, specifically radars and controllers. ATC is no longer viewed as a single agent; instead, there are two classes of agents—the air traffic control computer system and the controllers. The air traffic control system has as one of its subfunctions a process called Ensure-on-Course, which examines the location of the aircraft and compares it against the aircraft's expected location. If the two locations differ to a sufficient degree, ATC attempts to affect a course change, changing the location of the aircraft.

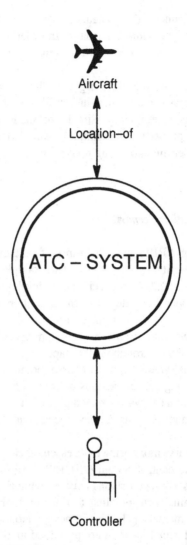

Figure 3. Initial context diagram of ATC system.

Now the system determines the locations of the aircraft as follows. The radar observes the aircraft and transmits a set of radar messages, indicating that targets have been observed at particular locations. A `Track-Correlation` function inputs these radar messages and processes them to produce a set of tracks. Each track corresponds to a specific aircraft; the locations associated with the tracks are updated when new radar messages are received. Meanwhile, expected aircraft locations are now computed from the aircraft flight plans, which in turn are input by the controllers. The `Ensure-on-Course` process is now modified so that it issues notifications to the controller (by signaling `Must-Change-Course` for an aircraft); the controller then issues commands to the aircraft over the radio.

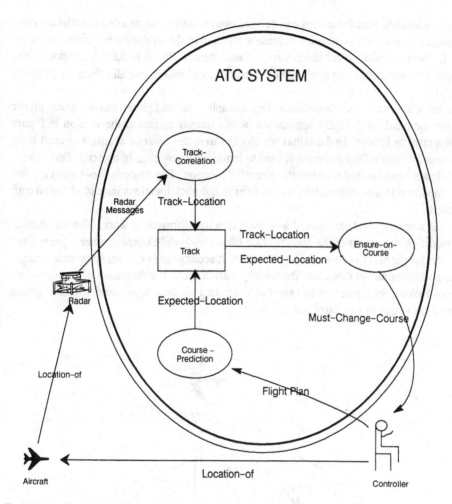

Figure 4. Detailed context diagram of the ATC system.

In order to get to this more detailed level of description, a number of transformations must be performed. Most of the transformations have to do with defining the pattern of data flow through the system. We can suggest three options for obtaining this more detailed description.

First, we can maintain a limited, very informal, link between the two descriptions—this, in fact, is what happens in most current practice. The detailed interconnections between abstractions are not stated explicitly and any attempt at traceability occurs at best through following a paper trail. It may be possible to say that description 2 follows description 1, but there is no record of the evolution (e.g., how as access to "location-of" data changed?) as we move toward a formal description.

Second, the interconnections can be manually derived and recorded—perhaps using a global replace command on a textual version of the stated information. Traceability is possible, but the process is tedious and error prone.

Third, evolution transformatons can be employed to derive the detailed description from the simplified one. We have implemented a number of the evolution transformations required. The user must select the desired transformations, but it is ARIES' responsibility to check the transformations applicability conditions and ensure that all effects are properly handled.

The most important transformation in this example is called Splice-Data-Accesses. Figure 5 shows the result of ARIES's application of this transformation to the version in Figure 3. It operates as follows. In the initial version `Ensure-On-Course` accesses aircraft locations directly. Splice-Data-Accesses is used to introduce a new class of object, called `Track`, which has a location that matches the aircraft's location. The `Ensure-On-Course` process is modified in a corresponding way to refer to the track locations instead of the aircraft locations.

This is a very typical example of how evolution transformations work. The transformation modifies one aspect of the specification (data flow) while keeping other aspects fixed (e.g., the functionality of `Ensure-On-Course`). It accomplishes this via systematic changes to the specification. In this case, the transformation scans the definition of `Ensure-On-Course` looking for references to `location-of`; each of these is replaced with a reference to the `Track-Location` attribute of tracks.

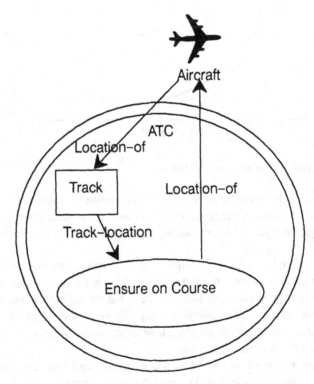

Figure 5. Intermediate context diagram of the ATC system.

Completing the derivation of this example requires further application of several transformations. Splice-Data-Accesses is applied again to introduce the object **Radar-Message**, which is an intermediate between **Aircraft** and **Track**. Maintain-Invariant-Reactively is invoked to construct processes for continuously updating the radar messages and the tracks. A transformation called Install-Protocol is used to introduce a notification protocol between the **Ensure-On-Course** process and the controller, so that **Ensure-On-Course** issues notifications to the controller whenever the location of the aircraft must be changed. A new process called **Course-Prediction** is added to compute expected locations from flight plans. Through this derivation the specification is gradually refined towards a version in which each system component interacts only with those data and agents that it will be able to interact with in the implemented system.

5. Conclusions Regarding the Specification Process

The experiments in specification development outlined above led to a number of conclusions regarding the nature of the specification development process. First, several central issues relating to specification development were identified: coordinating multiple users and viewpoints, capturing requirements that can be shared across systems, and sharing core concepts and knowledge across domains. Second, categories of stereotypic specification evolution steps were identified.

5.1. Central Issues

5.1.1. Coordinating Multiple Users and Viewpoints. The requirements for future air traffic control systems are extremely detailed: system descriptions for the AAS run into the hundreds of pages. The work of specification must be dividied among multiple analysts in order to be feasible. In our current attempts to formalize sections of the AAS requirements, we find that the functional areas that the FAA has identified for that system, such as track processing, flight plan processing, and traffic management, seem to be good candidates for assignment to different analysts or analyst teams.

One important conclusion was that a proper balance must be struck between coordinated and independent work of analysts. Requirements are not like program modules that can be handed off to independent coders to implement. Inevitably there is significant overlap between them. Requirements may share a significant amount of common terminology between them. Requirements expressed in one functional area may have impact on other functional areas. In the AAS specification, we specified track processing, flight plan processing, and assignment of control separately. We found that flight plan information had an impact on how tracks are disambiguated and that the process of handing off control of aircraft from one facility to the next had an impact on when flight plan information is communicated between facility computer systems. But rather than force analysts to constantly coordinate whenever an area of potential common concern was identified, we needed a way to allow analysts to work separately and merge their results.

Inconsistency Is Pervasive. Separate development of different requirements areas inevitably leads to inconsistencies. These inconsistencies are a natural consequence of allowing analysts to focus on different concerns individually. Although consistency is an important goal for the requirements process to achieve, we conclude that it cannot be guaranteed and maintained throughout the requirements analysis process without forcing analysts to constantly compare their requirements descriptions against each other. Therefore, consistency must be achieved gradually, at an appropriate point in the specification development process. Nevertheless, it may not be possible to recognize all inconsistencies within a system description.

Multiple Models Must be Supported. One place where inconsistencies need to be resolved is where multiple models are used. Our study of the road traffic control problem identified a need for supporting multiple models of concepts. A similar need was found in the air traffic control domain. When analyzing radar processing requirements it is important to model the dynamics of aircraft motion to make sure that the system is able to track aircraft under normal maneuver conditions. When specifying flight plan monitoring, however, it is sufficient to assume that aircraft will move in straight lines from point to point, and change direction instantaneously, since the time required for a maneuver is very short compared to the time typically spent following straight flight paths. One way of resolving such conflicts is to develop a specialization hierarchy that relates these models to common abstractions.

5.1.2. Sharing Requirements Across Systems.
The designer of an air traffic control system must make sure that computers and human agents can together achieve the goals of air traffic control, i.e., to ensure the safe, orderly, and expeditious flow of air traffic. How this will be done by AAS is, to some extent, determined by current air traffic control practice. Thus the next generation of controller consoles are being designed to simulate on computer displays the racks of paper flight strips that controllers currently use to keep track of flights. However, although air traffic control practice is codified in federal regulations and letters of agreement, and is thus resistant to change, the division of labor between computer and human controller is expected to change over time. The FAA anticipates that new computer systems will gradually be introduced into the new air traffic control framework over the next 20 years, taking increasing responsibility for activities that are now performed by controllers. Therefore, it is important to be able to represent the overall requirements on air traffic control without being forced to commit to particular computer systems satisfying those requirements. The requirements can then be carried forward to each successive computer system. Air traffic control thus serves as a useful case study in how requirements stated in terms of the domain are realized in specifications of software systems.

5.1.3. Sharing Across Domains.
Just as there are opportunities for sharing across systems in the same domain, there are opportunities for sharing across domains. The road traffic control problem shares certain characteristics with air traffic control: both problems are concerned with the maintenance of safe, orderly, and expeditious flow of vehicular traffic.

They both assume a common body of underlying concepts, such as vehicles, sensors, spatial geometry, etc. We have been endeavoring to model such concepts so that the commonalities across the two domains are captured, as well as the differences.

We are also modeling system concepts that apply to a range of computer systems, independent of domain. For example, an air traffic control system must maintain a database of flight plans. As such, it incorporates a variety of concerns common to any database system, such as how to enter and update such information, when to store and archive it, who has write access to the database, etc. These concerns are not shared with the road traffic control system, which does not maintain a database.

5.2. Typical Modifications

We are discovering important categories of specification modification. These categories are enabling us to provide adequate automation for all aspects of specification development and are providing insight into finding and encoding cornerstone decisions of a typical development.

5.2.1. Categorization by Focus of Change.
Our experience has revealed that the choice of which evolution transformation to apply is often determined by the nature of the change we wish to achieve. For example, we may recognize that the specification is inaccurate with respect to data flow and to correct this would apply an evolution transformation that would make the appropriate change to the specification's data flow.

We have identified the following important characteristics of specifications that people reason about and manipulate during design.

- The modular organizatin of the specification (e.g., which modules are components of some other module)
- The entity-relationship model of the specification (e.g., specialization among types, events, etc.), the signatures (formal parameters) of procedures, functions, relations, etc.)
- The data flow of the specification
- The information flow of the specification
- Control flow (e.g., the procedures invoked by a body of code)

5.2.2. Informal to Formal Mappings.
Analysts will frequently refer to existing documents for clarification or endorsement of requirements statements. The link between paragraphs in documents and resulting specifications either goes unstated or has only rudimentary machine mediation. As we describe below, hyperstrings are used in ARIES to capture informal and semiformal information. We can employ hyperstrings in evolutionary formalization as follows. First, we can introduce hyperstrings as attributes of specification objects, and gradually replace them with formal attributes with the same meaning. Second, we can parse the hyperstrings, looking for the names of objects, and replace the names with pointers to the objects. This parsing process is similar to the Intelligent Notepad of the KBRA. But whereas the Intelligent Notepad would immediately attempt to find object names in text, and sometimes make mistakes on poorly worded text, this parsing process is under more direct user control.

5.2.3. General to Specific Mappings. One common technique is to define a concept first by placing it at a high point in the specialization hierarchies, and describing informally what additional properties the concept should have. After browsing the knowledge base further, specializations that are closer to the analyst's intent may be found or else existing specializations may be adapted using evolution transformations. This allows the analyst to position the concept further down in the hierarchy. Through this process concepts can be gradually moved to their proper place in the hierarchy. We are interested in providing automated assistance here, using constraint propagation techniques to associate constraints with concepts and then finding specializations in the knowledge base that match those constraints.

5.2.4. Default Removal. The third opportunity for incremental formalization is in eliminating defaults. Many requirements, particularly nonfunctional ones, apply to a system by default unless specified otherwise. Defaults are also useful to support rapid construction of executable prototypes as many details must be filled in in a system description in order for it to be executable. A system description that is more detailed so that defaulting is no longer necessary can be viewed as more formal than one in which defaults are liberally employed.

5.2.5. Requirements to be Compromised. In many cases the initial requirements are overly ideal, and in the course of development they must be carefully compromised to make them mutually compatible. Traceability must record when (and why) such compromises occur. Since compromises to requirements are evolutions, we use our same mechanism—evolution transformations—to carry them out and record the applications of these transformations to provide traceability. It is difficult to predict ahead of time all the ramifications of interacting requirements. Instead, they can be uncovered through the process of incorporating the requirements into a specification and beginning the process of converting that specification into a more implementation-oriented form. In the case of requirements expressed as global constraints on behavior, this is done by taking the requirements and distributing them throughout the specification as locally expressed constraints. Once localized, the interaction between a requirement and its context can easily be determined, and means for circumventing conflicting interactions are often readily apparent.

6. An Outline of Our Specification Semantics

As the above description suggests, managing the evolution of specifications requires a deep semantic model of specifications. Before we can present our specification development tools in detail, it is necessary to give an overview of the underlying semantic model of specifications in ARIES. This model is based on the Gist specification language, [3], generalized to support requirements and reuse issues more readily. The semantic model is represented in ARIES as a set of specification component types and attributes, called the ARIES Metamodel.

The basic units of system descriptions in ARIES are *types, instances, relations, events,* and *invariants.*

6.1. Types, Instances, and Relations

The treatment of types, instances, and relations is compatible with most object-oriented approaches to requirements engineering (e.g., that of Hagelstein [16]). However, our entity-relationship model is more general and expressive than most, in order to support a wide range of entity-relationship notations. For those readers who are familiar with such systems, the following list summarizes the specific features that our entity-relationship system supports.

- Each type can have multiple subtypes and supertypes.
- Each instance can belong to any number of types simultaneously.
- Relations hold among any types of objects—there is no restriction that those types be primitive with respect to any particular machine representation.
- Relations need not be binary but can have arbitrary arity.
- Relations are fully associative—there is no need for separate relations to record the inverse of a given relation.

6.2. Events

System descriptions can describe behavior over time, modeled as a linear sequence of states. Each state is described fully in terms of what instances exist, what relations hold between them, and what events are active.

Events subsume all system processes and external events described as part of a system description. Events have duration, possibly spanning multiple states in a behavior and involving multiple entities of the system. Events can have preconditions, postconditions, and methods consisting of procedural steps. They may be explicitly activated by other events, or may occur spontaneously when their preconditions are met. They may have inputs and outputs.

Not all interactions with an event must occur through its input and output ports. It is often useful to describe events initially without concern for the specific inputs and outputs. For example, the early version of the `Ensure-On-Course` event described in Section 4.2 observed aircraft directly and modified their locations. An aircraft cannot be considered an "input" in the conventional sense here. Event declarations whose purpose is to describe activity rather than specify particular artifacts tend to have this flavor. We use the term *information flow* to refer to any transfer of information between agents and their environment. With these terms in mind, the transformation example in Sectin 4.2 can be understood as transforming idealized information flows into concrete data flows.

6.3. Invariants

Invariants are predicates that must hold during all states in the system. Invariants are divided into subclasses, according to their intended function. *Domain axioms* are predicates about the environment that are assumed to hold, such as the configuration of airspaces. These invariants will hold regardless of what the system being specified might or might not do. *Functional constraints* are invariants involving the system being specified, or which are to be guaranteed by the system being specified. They are thus a kind of functional requirement, and must be explicitly implemented or respected in the system being specified. An example of such a constraint is the requirement that aircraft not deviate from their designated courses by more than a set amount. Dependency links are established during the analysis process between such requirements and the events or other specification components (e.g., `Ensure-On-Course`) that are intended to satisfy them.

Specification components have associated with them a variety of attributes, including nonfunctional ones. Nonfunctional attributes are treated as relations. Specific mathematical, logical entailment, or engineering trade-off formulas that constrain system designs are a form of invariant that constrains the static properties of specific system instances.

6.4. Comparison to Other Knowledge-Based Systems

ARIES is compatible with a variety of other knowledge-based systems. At the present time the notation that we use most frequently for building a knowledge base is Reusable Gist, which is derived from the Gist specification language [3], with some constructs borrowed from Refine[3] and Loom [28]. However, ARIES can also input and output significant subsets of pure Refine and input knowledge bases written in Loom. Fortunately, analysts do not need to make extensive use of any of these knowledge engineering notations; they may manipulate graphical notations instead, and request natural-language paraphrases of knowledge-based components. The main conclusion that we hope the reader draws from this discussion is that most important requirements notations can be captured in this framework.

7. Mechanisms for Supporting Specification Evolution

In this section, we describe the major technical challenges we have undertaken to create ARIES.

7.1. Folders and Workspaces

A major concern in ARIES is providing an organizational structure for specifications and their underlying conceptual models, so that groups of analysts can collaborate in specification development. The primary units of organization are *workspaces* and *folders*. Each analyst interacting with ARIES has one or more private workspaces, which are collections of system descriptions that are to be interpreted in a common context. Whenever an analyst is working on a problem, it is in the context of a particular workspace of definitions appropriate for that problem. In order to populate a workspace, the analyst makes use of one or more folders, which are collections of reusable concept definitions. The ARIES knowledge base currently contains 122 folders comprising over 1500 concepts. Folders may contain either formal or informal descriptions. Reusable formal descriptions include precise definitions of reusable concepts; reusable informal descriptions include excerpts from published documents describing requirements of the domain, e.g., air traffic control manuals.

Figures 6 and 7 give a view of those folders used in the road traffic control problem. The uppermost folder in the hierarchy of folders created for this problem is called **shared-tlp**; this folder contains common domain terminology to be used throughout the project. Figure 6 lists the reusable folders that this folder inherits from. At the highest level are domain-independent descriptions of commonly occurring concepts, such as people and

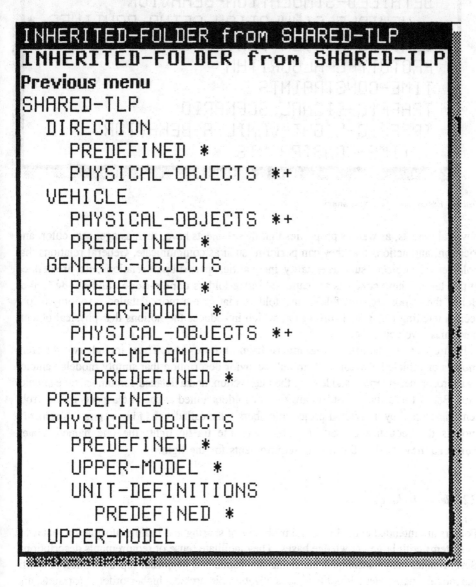

Figure 6. Folders inherited by **shared-tlp**.

```
INHERITED-FOLDER from SHARED-TLP
INHERITED-FOLDER from SHARED-TLP
Previous menu
SHARED-TLP
   VEHICLE-SIMULATION-SETUP-ROUTINES
   DETAILED-SIMULATION-BEHAVIOR
      VEHICLE-SIMULATION-SETUP-ROUTINES  *
   VEHICLE-SIMULATION-DEFINITIONS
   PROTOTYPE-ALGORITHM
   TIME-CONSTRAINTS
   TRAFFIC-SIGNAL-SCENARIO
   TRAFFIC-LIGHT-VANILLA-BEHAVIOR
      TIME-CONSTRAINTS  *
```

Figure 7. Folders that inherit from **shared-tlp**.

physical objects, as well as properties that these objects have, such as age, sex, color, and location, and actions that they can perform, such as communicate. General relations that hold between objects, such as equality, inequalities, part-subpart relations, etc. are defined at this level. These concepts are captured in the folders **upper-model** and **predefined**. Below these most general folders are folders that give a more detailed taxonomy of objects, including **physical-objects**, which introduces the notions that physical objects have mass, velocity, etc.

Figure 7 shows the folders that inherit from **shared-tlp**. These include two different models of vehicle behavior: a "vanilla" behavior description that simply models vehicles as approaching, entering, and leaving the intersection, and a detailed continuous time simulation. Below these shared folders are further folders aimed at specific aspects of the problem, developed by individual project members. One called **traffic-signal-scenario** models the sequence of state transitions of the traffic light; the one named **time-constraints** models the timing requirements for the light.

7.2. Reuse Techniques

Folders are intended to deal with the problems of sharing and hiding information that arise in systems with large knowledge bases. They facilitate reuse of requirements descriptions. Several other reuse techniques are being developed and explored: representation of multiple models, parameterized folders, specialization hierarchies, higher-order constraints, and transformations.

7.2.1. Representation of Multiple Models. Analysts may selectively incorporate models of concepts into their specifications, as in the following example. The ARIES knowledge base contains several alternative models for directions: as compass points (e.g., North, South, East, and West), as the number of degrees clockwise from magnetic North, or as multiples of 10 degrees from magnetic North (used to mark the direction of runways). Figure 8 illustrates the taxonomic relationship among these models.

folder direction
exports {
    type direction specialization-of ordered-value
    }
inherits {predefined}

folder named-direction
exports {
    type named-direction
        specialization-of direction;
    var east:named-direction;
    var north:named-direction;
    var south:named-direction;
    var west:named-direction
    }
uses {direction}

folder navigational-direction
exports {
    type compass-point
        specialization-of integer
        specialization-of direction;
    type azimuth
        specialization-of compass-point;
    invariant compass-range
        ∀ (cp : compass-point) $0 \leq cp \land cp < 360$
    }
uses {direction;predefined}

folder aircraft-direction
exports {
    type runway-orientation
        specialization-of direction;
    invariant runway-range
        ∀ (ro: runway-orientation)
        $1 \leq ro$ and $ro \leq 36$
} uses {direction; predefined}

Figure 8. ARIES contains several models for the "direction" concept.

Clearly, a model of directions used to mark runways is not well suited to road traffic control problems (although it might be employed in coordinating ground traffic at airports). In **shared-tlp** the decision was recorded to model direction in the road traffic control problem as named compass points. This is accomplished as follows. The folder containing models of direction, called **direction**, contains both a generic concept of direction, also called **direction**, and each of the various models of direction. The model of direction as compass points is called **named-direction**. The administrator of the **shared-tlp** folder defines the concept **direction** locally as a renamed version of the concept **named-direction** taken from the **direction** folder. Then whenever project members use the concept **direction** they will use the local version rather than the more general version. ARIES continues to record that the local version of **direction** is a specialization of the general **direction**, so any attributes of that generic concept will apply to the specific concept as well.

7.2.2. Parameterized Specifications. As part of our current research we are investigating the use of parameterized specifications. Parameterized specifications are folders whose contents contain free variables, which must be bound when the folder is used. An example of such a folder is the folder **tracker-concepts**, which defines concepts related to tracking, such as trajectories, location prediction, and smoothing. This folder contains a free variable **tracked-object-type**, which is the type of the object being tracked (e.g., **aircraft**). Such folders are used by instantiating a copy of the folder with the variables bound, e.g., specifying that the value of **tracked-object-type** is **aircraft**. The result is the definition of a tracker of aircraft positions. Such parameterized specifications are an important mechanism for representing requirements cliches, and are similar to the approach of the Requirements Apprentice [33].

There is a strong coupling between parameterized specifications and transformations. Many transformations introduce specification constructs having a stereotypic form: Splice-Data-Accesses is one such transformation. The form of the intermediate object created by this transformation can be stored in a folder and instantiated as needed. We expect to make increasing use of such parameterized specifications in our transformation library.

7.2.3. Reuse Through Specialization. If an analyst needs to define a new concept, it is often advantageous to define it as a specialization of one or more abstract concepts, rather than construct a definition from scratch. As the direction example in the previous section illustrates, concepts are organized into specialization hierarchies at the same time that they are organized into folders. The specialization hierarchies relate specific concepts to more general concepts, as in other knowledge-based systems. They also relate specific models of concepts to generic models of the same concepts. ARIES uses specialization hierarchies more extensively than common knowledge representation languages: it supports specialization hierarchies for relations and events as well as types. These extended specialization hierarchies provide more opportunities for knowledge reuse. Several important technical concerns had to be addressed in order to ensure that such specialization hierarchies are meaningful.

Specialization hierarchies establish subsumption relations between terms. That is, given two concepts S and T, S is a specialization of T if the following is true:

$$\forall(x)\ S(x)\ \Rightarrow\ T(x).$$

Specialization hierarchies of relations and events are defined in a similar manner. If we have two binary relations $R(x, y)$ and $S(x, y)$, R is a specialization of S if

$$\forall(x, y)\ R(x, y) \Rightarrow S(x, y).$$

Unfortunately, the above definition of specialization only makes sense when the specialization and the generalization have the same number of parameters, and parameters correspond. With multiple-arity relations and events, developed at different levels of abstraction, this is rarely the case.

Consider, for example, two events, **takeoff** and **move**. Intuitively, it would make sense for **takeoff** to be a specialization of **move**: if an aircraft is taking off, it is also moving. However, the two events are likely to have different parameters. In the ARIES model, **takeoff** takes as input one parameter, the aircraft taking off. Event **move**, on the other hand, has three parameters: the object being moved, the agent doing the moving, and the location that the object will be moved to. A simple logical implication between the two concepts cannot be drawn, because the parameters of the two concepts do not match up.

The solution to this problem that we provide in ARIES is to *reify* the events and relations, i.e., to treat instances of them as objects. When an event starts, an object representing the event is created; when the event completes, the object is destroyed. Parameters of the events become attributes of the corresponding event objects. Subsumption for events and relations is then equivalent to type subsumption for the objects representing the events and relations.[4]

In the case of **takeoff** and **move**, subsumption is defined as follows. Figure 9 shows definitions of **takeoff** and **move** in Reusable Gist. Move actions are represented as objects with three attributes: **actor**, **actee**, and **destination**. These are the names of the input parameters in the declaration of **move**. Takeoff actions are modeled as having four parameters and roles. One of them, **ac**, is an input parameter—the aircraft taking off. Another, **destination**, is an output parameter, bound to the aircraft's new location when the takeoff is completed. Two other roles, **actee** and **actor**, are bound to the value of the input parameter **ac**. (Note that these bindings are specified in the **roles** attribute of **takeoff**.) When a takeoff event is initiated, a corresponding object is created, with attributes **ac**, **actor**, **actee**, and **destination**, corresponding to the parameters and roles. By the semantics of term subsumption, making **takeoff** a specialization of **move** means that every event object describing a takeoff must also be a well-formed **move** object.

```
event takeoff[ac : aircraft]
    outputs (destination := ac.location-of)
    roles (actee := ac, actor := ac)
    specialization-of move
    precondition ac.location-of is-a ground-location
    postcondition ac.location-of is-a air-location ∧ in-flight(ac)

event move [actor:agent, actee:physical-object, desitnation:location]
    precondition ¬ location-of(actee,destination)
    postcondition location-of(actee,destination)
```

Figure 9. Definitions of takeoff and move.

Note that when an event is a specialization of another event, it must inherit the preconditions and postconditions of the events that it is a specialization of. Thus, `takeoff` inherits the precondition and postcondition of `move`, meaning that the location of the aircraft at the end of the takeoff is different from that at the beginning of the takeoff. Importantly, this serves as an additional consistency check, something that is useful when we define methods for some of these events. Suppose that an analyst describes the procedure for takeoff, which includes receiving clearance from the controller. If the clearance is denied, the takeoff is aborted. But now the declared specialization hierarchy is inconsistent with the conditions on `move`: it is possible to "execute" the `takeoff` procedure and have no move occur. We believe that the creation, detection, and resolution of such inconsistency is central to the specification development process. In this case, to remove the inconsistency, an analyst could define a specialization of `takeoff` called `successful-takeoff`, and make `successful-takeoff` the specialization of `move` instead of `takeoff`.

7.2.4. Reuse of Higher-Order Properties. Our concern for codifying domain knowledge in a reusable form has led us to introduce higher-order constructs into our conceptual modeling language. Higher-order constructs are needed to define concepts that are defined over classes of other concepts, or that describe other concepts. In ARIES they are defined in terms of the types and relations in the ARIES Metamodel. It is often the case that an applciation-specific concept must satisfy some generic property expressed in higher-order terms; referring to the higher-order property can help ensure the accuracy of the application-specific definition.

A simple example of a concept that is defined over a class of concepts is the concept of a symmetric relation. The concept `symmetric` is defined as follows:

implicit relation symmetric(r:relation-declaration)
    iff
      arity(r, 2) $\wedge \forall$ (a:entity, b:entity) r(a,b) $\Leftrightarrow$ r(b,a)

This defines `symmetric` as a unary relation that holds for other relations. A relation r is symmetric if its arity is 2, and if for all objects a and b, if $r(a, b)$ is true then $r(b, a)$ is true.

Another example of a useful higher-order property is the property of a server satisfying requests in a first-come-first-served fashion. This property is higher order because it is a property that can hold for any process that handles and acts on requests, i.e., it is a property of a particular class of events. First-come-first-served is defined as a temporal relationship between requests and actions: if two requests of the same server are made in a particular order, the responses must be in the same order. This representation is amenable to automatic validation in executable simulations, although at this time we have not yet developed the monitoring tools for such temporal relationships.

7.2.5. Adaptations. The above techniques all enable analysts to construct new specifications by reusing portions of existing specifications and domain knowledge. Our experience suggests that it is unrealistic to expect all concepts to be used in a specification to be present in reusable form. Hence, reuse techniques must be complemented with techniques for adapting and modifying existing knowledge. Although informal reuse (i.e., cutting and pasting as in a text editor) is possible, we believe that there are many advantages to be gained by using evolution transformations to control this process. Evolution transformations make it possible to adapt concepts in the knowledge base in restricted, systematic ways, to avoid the introduction of errors during the adaptation process.

7.3. Acquisition and Review

In order to make use of folders and reusable information, it is necesary to be able to view them, select from them, and add to them. These actions are done through an interface called the Presentation Facility, which makes it possible to enter and view information through a variety of different notations.

7.3.1. Presentation Categories. All notations that ARIES supports are views of the same underlying system description representation. The notations, which we call "presentations," fall into the following categories.

1. Graphical presentations are diagrams showing certain objects in the ARIES knowledge base, and the links interconnecting them. The graphical presentations in ARIES include specialization hierarchy diagrams (such as in Figure 10), state transition diagrams, data or information flow diagrams, context diagrams such as those shown in Section 4.2, and functional decomposition diagrams. Many of these diagramming capabilities were also present in the KBRA system. In addition, we are considering other diagrams, such as entity-relation diagrams, STATECHART-like notations, and further information flow abstractions. Domain-specific presentations, such as the depiction of objects in a roadway scene or an airspace, are especially useful to make system descriptions understandable to noncomputer specialists, and we have been experimenting with these presentations as well.
2. Spreadsheet presentations, developed for KBRA, are tabular diagrams that allow analysts to enter requirements for a collection of components of the system description and interact with an underlying constraint propagation system which is maintaining dependency links among requirements statements.
3. Formal presentations are detailed formal specification texts, e.g., those written in Reusable Gist.
4. Natural language is used in initial acquisition to capture informal statements that will later be formalized. It is also used for checking formal specifications against informal requirements, in machine-generated requirements documents, and in explaining specifications to clients and others who are not experts in requirements modeling.

The engine for the natural language presentation is the ARIES Paraphraser. It translates formal internal representations into natural language descriptions. It is a useful explanation and training tool for presenting requirements and specifications to users who are unfamiliar

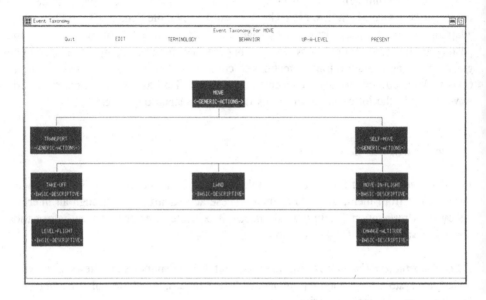

Figure 10. A taxonomy showing specializations of the "Move" event.

with the formalism. It is also a useful debugging aid for specifiers. Our representation permits the insertion of grammatical annotations and names to use in displaying objects, both of which permit better English translations to be generated by the Paraphraser. The following list shows an example of Paraphraser output, taken from a specification of an automated manufacturing task.

A robot R can transport a part P to a location DEST. To perform a transport, R sequentially does the following five steps.

1. R opens grasp.
2. R positions arm to the location of P.
3. R closes grasp.
4. R simultaneously (atomically) does the following two steps.
   (a) R positions arm to DEST.
   (b) R updates the location of P to DEST.
5. R opens grasp.

The paraphraser has undergone steady enhancement and extension of coverage for some years now; as a result, it has become a powerful, effective tool for presentation of specifications. Furthermore, because the ARIES Metamodel of specifications and the ARIES transformation library are part of the ARIES knowledge base, the paraphraser is also an important tool for on-line documentation. A user can, for example, apply the paraphraser to an evolution transformation in order to learn what it does.

7.3.2. Supporting Multiple Presentations. The key technical challenge in supporting multiple presentations has been to develop a common internal representation, the ARIES Metamodel, that will easily map to the notations of stereotypical views of systems (e.g., data flow arcs, system functional decomposition, state transitions, predicate calculuslike formalisms). Some metamodel concepts are relatively separable and easy to handle. For example, the type, relation, and event taxonomic diagrams are generated from the internal representation in an obvious way. Other concepts are highly interrelated. States are relations that are derived from a designated relation having a parameter varying over a finite set of values. State transitions are demon events that update the `current-state`—i.e., change the value of the parameter and place some aspect of the system in a new state. In Figure 11, `approach-int`, `leave-int`, and `enter-int` are all state-transition events. `Car-relative-location-approaching`, `car-relative-location-inside`, and `carp-relative-location-elsewhere` are relations for each of the three values—approaching, inside, and elsewhere—allowable for the relative-location type.

This means that arbitrary relations and events will not be presented in state transition diagrams, as they are not of the desired form. Instead, the state transition presentation only presents relations of class `state-relation`, i.e., those which are in a form similar to a `current-state` relation that would have been acquired as a state transition diagram. Conversely, `state-transitions` and `state-relations` will show up in other presentations. For example, a `state-transition` will appear in any Gist presentation as a demon, and along with other demons will populate various event presentations.

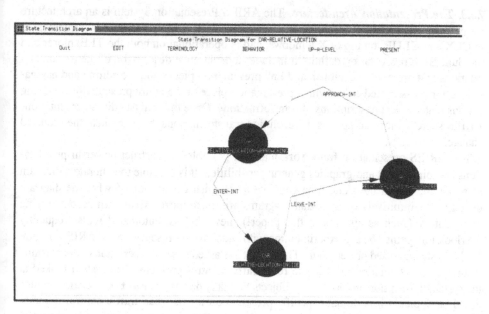

Figure 11. A state transition diagram that displays events and relations.

Another issue in supporting multiple presentations in ARIES is how to support system descriptions that contain a mixture of formal and informal information. The ARIES Metamodel tolerates missing information to a high degree. Such partial descriptions may not provide all of the information necessary to generate a particular presentation, in which case stub markers such as `unspecified` appear in the presentation. In other cases, defaults may be used to fill in the missing information. In addition, some of the presentations are designed with incompleteness in mind. For example, Reusable Gist differs both from the earlier Gist language and the Refine language in the extent to which it can express partial specifications.

Informal and formal information are integrated using a data structure called a *hyperstring*. Hyperstrings are text strings possibly containing pointers to other objects. We distinguish hyperstrings from hypertext, for the following reason. In most hypertext systems, such as Notecards [17], each piece of hypertext is a separate object. Each object has a name and a body where the text goes. In contrast, we wish to use hypertext as values for attributes, not as objects. Objects can have multiple hypertext attributes at the same time. For example, the definition of a concept `flying-aircraft` may be hypertext; likewise the name of concept itself can be hypertext, containing pointers to the concepts from which it is derived—`fly` and `aircraft`. System descriptions containing hyperstrings may be viewed through several presentations, but most commonly through the presentation called *structured text*. Structured text presents textual information hierarchically, showing the attributes of an object, the values of those attributes, and pointers to other objects within the hyperstring attributes.

7.3.3. The Presentation Architecture.
The ARIES Presentation System is an architecture for defining interactive presentations linked to the ARIES Metamodel. It is implemented in CLX and CLUE, on top of X windows, and is operational on both the TI Explorer and the Sun. Each presentation definition includes a declarative description of the metamodel relations that are used to establish and link presentation pieces and the editing and navigation actions (associated either with a presentation piece or the entire presentation). Editing actions match effect descriptions of transformations. Once the analyst edits a presentation, ARIES searches for and applies the evolution transformations that can make the required change.

The ARIES presentation framework makes it possible to construct powerful presentations combining text and graphics general capabilities. It is possible to generate a diagram of a system, and at the same time generate an English description of what the diagram depicts. It is intuitively obvious that diagrams are much more useful with accompanying commentary (such as appears in this paper!); nevertheless, automated tools frequently overlook this point. We are experimenting with such mixed presentations in ARIES. Figure 12 shows such a mixed presentation. The analyst has asked to see a description of the meaning of the `part-of` relation used in the road traffic control problem. The system looked at the system description and found two objects that take part in the `part-of` relation, which could be depicted in a domain-specific presentation for the road traffic control domain. A diagram was composed, and at the same time the Paraphraser was used to generate text describing the situation. The association between presentation objects and internal representation is declarative, so that the system can reason about what kinds of objects are presentable in a presentation when deciding what objects to present.

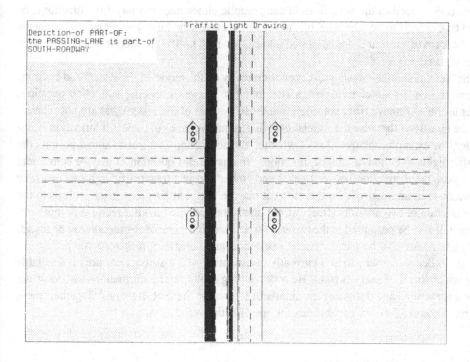

Figure 12. A mixed, domain-specific presentation.

7.4. Analysis and Simulation

Analysis tools include a constraint propagation engine and an incremental static analyzer. Analysis tools are important in order to check for completeness and consistency. A constraint mechanism, derived from Steele's Constraint Language [37], has been incorporated into ARIES for general maintenance of constraints—bidirectional propagation, contradiction detection, retraction, and explanation. This mechanism is essential where there are interacting design properties (e.g., interplay between performance characteristics) and developers can use assistance in identifying when an interaction of requirements may not be achievable. An incremental static analyzer, a version of the static analyzer developed for the Specification Assistant [26], maintains calling and type information for the system description as it is being edited. It also does such things as detect specification freedoms that must be removed temporarily before simulation can be performed.

Simulation tools are useful in order to observe the behavior of a proposed system or its environment in order to determine appropriate parameters for requirements or to discover unexpected or erroneous behavior. Simulation of vehicle behavior demonstrates, for example, how long it takes for traffic flow to return to normal after a light has changed, thus suggesting what the appropriate light duration should be based on the rate of traffic flow.

Simulations are constructed by means of a specially modified compiler that translates a subset of the ARIES Metamodel into Lisp and AP5, an in-core relational database [10].

Events described in the specification can compile either into ordinary Lisp functions, or into task objects to be scheduled by the simulator's task scheduler. Functional requirements in the form of invariants are compiled into rules which notify the analyst if and when they are violated [5].

Successful simulation analysis depends crucially on the model of the system and environment chosen for simulation. When attempting to answer a specific validation question, it is useful to remove from consideration those features of the system that are not relevant to the question otherwise the simulation will generate volumes of useless information. Consider, for example, the question of whether a specification of a traffic signal permits the traffic lights to be red in all four directions. To answer this question, it may be convenient to ignore the distinction between green and amber and just treat traffic lights as two-state devices—red and nonred. Furthermore, it may be useful at first to restrict analysis to the intersection of two one-way streets: if red lights are permitted in all directions in this case, they will also be permitted in the two-way street case. If a suitable abstraction can be found, validation can also be performed by inspection and constraint propagation.

Kevin Benner in our group is currently investigating which abstractions are most suitable for which kinds of analysis tasks. He is developing evolution transformations that construct the abstractions and designing the simulator to execute these abstractions. Together, these form a powerful set of capabilities for specification validation.

7.5. Evolution Transformations

As part of our earlier KBSA work, we built a sizable library of evolution transformations, that is, transformations whose very purpose is to *change* the meaning of the specification to which they are applied. Like conventional correctness-preserving transformations, they blend computer power—the ability to conduct repeated, mechanical operations rapidly and reliably—and human intuition—knowing which transformation to apply when. Transformations allow us to build specifications incrementally, explain specifications incrementally, i.e., by going through the incremental record of their construction, and modify specifications by applying further evolutions.

In the ARIES project we are now addressing several deficiencies in our earlier development. The focus of the KBSA project was to make an initial exploration of this approach to specification construction and validation. Thus, in populating our library of evolution transformations, we were motivated by the examples we studied (primarily those of a patient monitoring system, and a portion of an air-traffic control system). We built somewhat generalized versions of the evolution transformations necessary for these examples, but paid little attention to completeness or uniformity of our emerging library. We subdivided the library into categories of transformations (e.g., data-flow-modifying transformations, structure-adding transformations) but otherwise did little to support the user of the system in selecting the appropriate transformation. In ARIES we address all of these deficiencies.

7.5.1. Infrastructure to Support Evolution. A major goal of the ARIES project has been to support the user in selecting evolution transformations from a library, and in applying them. This library constitutes reusable knowledge about the *process* of requirements analysis, which complements the knowledge about the inputs and outputs of this process, i.e., knowledge of domains and systems. We now sketch the approach we are taking toward developing a usable evolution transformation library.

The representation of specification concepts enables efficient and effective modification of the semantic content of complex specifications. Having identified specification characteristics, we then chose a common representation for them, semantic nets—nodes connected by links, where the types of the nodes and links determine which characteristic they represent. For example, in the entity-relationship model, procedures and types will be represented by nodes; the type of a procedure's formal parameter is represented by linking the node representing that procedure with the node representing that type. Changes to the specification induce the corresponding changes on these semantic net representations of the specification's characteristics. Each change can be expressed as a combination of creating and destroying nodes, and inserting and removing links between nodes. We have identified frequently recurring composites of these operations, for example, *splice* removes a direct link between two nodes, A and B say, and replaces it with two links via an intermediary, e.g., C, so that A is linked to C and C is linked to B.

Finally, we characterized each evolution transformation in terms of the effects it induces on the semantic net representation of each of the above categories. Splice-Data-Accesses, illustrated in Section 4.2, is an example of a transformation that performs a splice along the information flow dimension. Likewise, an evolution transformation that introduces an intermediate specialization of some concept (e.g., given a specification containing type person and type airline pilot, a specialization of person, we might introduce an intermediate type employed person) is characterized as inducing a *splice* on the specialization link structure. Similarly, an evolution transformation that wraps a statement inside a conditional is also characterized as inducing a *splice* but on the control-flow structure (the control flow link that led into the original statement now leads into the surrounding conditional statement, and there is a link from the conditional to the original statement).

These steps considerably improved the use and organization of our library of transformations in the following ways:

1. Selection from the library—to select an evolution transformation, we give the characteristics of the changes we wish to induce on the specification, expressed as generic operations on the different characteristics of specifications. We distinguish between changes that we want to have happen, changes that we do not want to have happen, and changes that we do not care about.
2. Coverage of the library—we can (crudely) estimate where our library lacks coverage by looking for useful combinations of generic changes on the different characteristics for which there are not evolution transformations that induce those changes.
3. Uniformity of the library—seemingly unrelated evolution transformations that induce the same generic changes on different characteristics can be seen to be similar, and are constructed to reflect this similarity.

In addition to augmenting the evolution transformations with generic descriptions of the effects they induce, we also augment them with explicit representations of their inputs (what they must be given), outputs (what new specification structure(s) they produce), and preconditions (what conditions must be true to guarantee that they will run correctly). These are represented in the same internal representation that ARIES uses for describing inputs, outputs, and constraints on events. Each aspect of the transformation may also be given a hypertext documentation string, as is customary for other concept definitions in the system. This makes it possible to employ the same presentation and explanation tools to transformations as are applicable to components of application system descriptions.

Figure 13 shows machine generated documentation for the Splice-Data-Accesses transformation. It shows a number of attributes associated with the transformation; their meaning is as follows. Concept descriptions are informal descriptions of what the concept means; any concept in the ARIES knowledge base may have a concept description associated with it. Notes are warnings to potential users of the concept or transformation; in this case, the warning points out that Splice-Data-Accesses performs several changes in addition to splicing. Input parameters, output parameters, and preconditions play the same role with transformations that they play with any other events. Goals are conditions that the transformation is intended to achieve; they form part of the postcondition of the event. They differ from ordinary postconditions in that if they are already satisfied at the time the transformation is attempted, the transformation is skipped. Main effects describe the effects of the transformation along the various semantic dimensions.

7.6. Traceability

As indicated in Section 2.1, traceability is an essential characteristic of requirements specifications. Evolution transformations improve evolvability of specifications; this creates an even greater need for traceability support. Our main approach to providing traceability is to keep the record of the applications of the transformations and their effect (both evolution transformations, and conventional correctness-preserving transformations). This record links requirements to derived specifications, and ultimately to implementations. Notice that our characterization of the effects of transformations in terms of specification characteristics (data flow, control flow, etc.) is crucial to tracing the realization of a variety of kinds of formal requirements expressed in terms of these characteristics.

Transformation histories are best suited for recording how a specification was developed. In many cases, what is more important is what a specification was developed from, and why. Therefore, some transformations retain a copy of the original untransformed specification component and record an association between the old version and the new version. This is particularly useful for relating external informal documents to system descriptions.

7.7. Reconciling Conflicting Views

ARIES permits views of specifications to diverge, via different folders. Although divergence is important at certain stages of the analysis process, such divergences must eventually be reconciled. One technique that we have explored to facilitate reconciliation is the process of merging parallel elaborations [12]. Feather analyzed a restricted case of reconciliation where different views of the specification are all derived by transformation from a common root specification that describes the system in a very abstract way. Feather's technique is to attempt to replay the various transformations in a linear sequence. By analyzing

Splice-Data-Accesses: Transformation
Concept description: Splice a data object into the information access path from an object to an agent or activity. The transformation may be applied when the agent or activity, called **Accessor**, accesses some relation **Accessed-Relation**, which is an attribute of some object **Accessed-Object**. The transformation modifies the definition of **Accessor** so that it does not access **Accessed-Relation** anymore. It does this as follows. It creates a new type **Intermediary-Object**, with a new attribute **Intermediary-Rel**, which correspond to **Accessed-Object** and **Accessed-Relation**, respectively. Every reference to **Accessed-Relation** in **Accessor** is replaced with a reference to **Intermediary-Rel**. The result is a specification with the same behavior as before, but with a different pattern of information flow. *Note:* This transformation creates a new type and new relations. If you want instead to modify existing types or relations, you may wish to use the more general transformation **Generalized-Splice**.

Input parameters:
  Accessor: Entity:
      Component currently accessing the relation
  Accessed-Relation: Entity:
      Relation currently being accessed directly
  Accessed-Object: Entity:
      Object type that **Accessed-Relation** is an attribute of
  Intermediary-Object-Type-Name: Entity:
      Name of type of intermediary object
  Intermediary-Rel-Name: Entity:
      Name of new object's relation, to be accessed instead of **Accessed-Relation**
  Correspondence-Rel-Name: Entity:
      Name of new relation mapping old object to new data object
Object parameters:
  Intermediary-Object:
      New object type, named **Intermediary-Object-Type-Name**
  Intermediary-Rel:
      New object's relation, to be accessed instead of **Accessed-Relation**
  Correspondence-Rel:
      New relation mapping old object to the intermediary object
Precondition: The **Accessor** must be an event or type declaration.
Goal: The **Accessor** does not access the **Accessed-Relation**.
Main effects:
  A **Accesses-Fact** relation between **Accessor** and **Accessed-Relation** is spliced.
  A **Type-Declaration** named **Intermediary-Object** is created.
  A **Relation-Declaration** named **Intermediary-Rel** is created.
  A **Relation-Declaration** named **Correspondence-Rel** is created.

Figure 13. Machine-generated documentation for Splice-Data-Accesses.

the transformations, their applicability conditions, and what they apply to, it is possible in many cases to determine automatically whether transformations applied to different views may interfere with each other.

ARIES also exploits parallelism in development, but not necessarily in the manner assumed above. With ARIES analysts construct private folders that may not be transformed versions of the shared folders. In the road traffic control problem, e.g., the shared folders contain shared definition of concepts, not shared abstract specifications of the traffic controller. Furthermore, the relationship of shared to private is not always abstract to detailed. In some cases, just the reverse arises. Our current work on constructing abstracted versions of specifications for validation, described in Section 7.4, is producing examples of this. It can be useful to remove detail in order to investigate validation questions; likewise, it is also useful to remove detail in order to facilitate specification of requirements in the first place. The more detail that is provided in reusable knowledge, the more need there will be to suppress this detail to make specification easier. An analyst may also deliberately suppress detail in order to avoid making the system requirements excessively dependent on those details. Reconciliation difficulties also occur when analysts have each chosen alternative, incompatible models of the same concept.

The approach that we envision for ARIES centers of gradual elimination of differences between the conceptual models, regardless of their origin. If two members of an analysis team are using conflicting definitions of the same concept, they will each employ transformations step by step to eliminate those differences. In some cases this will involve having each analyst distribute the transformations that they employed so that the other analysts can employ them as well. As differences are resolved, specification components can be gradually promoted to the project-shared folders. In cases where an analyst has employed a model that is more detailed than necessary for the shared model, abstraction transformations may be employed to reduce the detail to the level shared throughout the project.

8. Related Work

The evolutionary approach to requirements specification has a number of precursors. Burstall and Goguen [8] argued that complex specifications should be put together from simple ones, and developed their language CLEAR to provide a mathematical foundation for this construction process. They recognized that the construction process itself has structure, employs a number of repeatedly used operations, and is worthy of explicit formalization and support—a position that we agree with wholeheartedly.

Goldman observed that natural language descriptions of complex tasks often incorporate an evolutionary vein—the final description can be viewed as an elaboration of some simpler description, itself the elaboration of a yet simpler description, etc., back to some description deemed sufficiently simple to be comprehended from a nonevolutionary description [14]. He identified three "dimensions" of changes between successive descriptions: *structural*—concerning the amount of detail the specification reveals about each individual state of the process, *temporal*—concerning the amount of change between successive states revealed by the specification, and *coverage*—concerning the range of possible behaviors permitted by a specification. We were motivated by these observations about description to try to apply such an evolutionary approach to the *construction* of specifications.

Fickas [13] suggested the application of an artificial intelligence (AI) problem-solving approach to specification construction. Fundamental to his approach is the notion that the steps of the construction process can be viewed as the primitive operations of a more general problem-solving process, and are hence ultimately mechanizable. Continuing work in this direction is reported in [1] and [35].

In the Programmer's Apprentice project (see [34] and, more recently, [39]), the aim—to build a tool that will act as an intelligent assistant to a skilled programmer—focuses on a different part of the software development activity from the focus of our work, yet much of what they have found has relevance to our enterprise. In their approach, programs are constructed by combining algorithmic fragments stored in a library. These algorithmic fragments are expressed using a sophisticated plan representation, with the resulting benefit of being readily combinable and identifiable. Their more recent project on supporting requirements acquisition (the "Requirements Apprentice," [33]) addresses the early stages of the software development process and includes similar techniques to those of the Programmer's Apprentice but operating on representations of requirements. Use of the Programmer's Apprentice is thus centered around selection of the appropriate fragment and its composition with the growing program, with application of minor transformations to tailor these introduced fragments. In contrast, our approach has been centered around selection of the appropriate evolution transformations and reformulating abstract descriptions of system behavior using such transformations. Yet, in fact, the two approaches are closely related. Many evolution transformations instantiate cliches as part of their function. We are currently exploring ways of making these cliches more explicit in our transformation system.

Karen Huff has developed a software process modeling and planning system that is in some ways similar to ours [20]. Her GRAPPLE language for defining planning operators influenced our representation of evolution transformations. Conversely, her meta-operators applying to process plans were influenced by our work on evolution transformations.

Kelly and Nonnenmann's WATSON system [27] constructs formal specifications of telephone system behavior from informal scenarios expressed in natural language. Their system formalizes the scenarios and then attempts to incrementally generalize the scenario in order to produce a finite-state machine. Their system is able to assume significant initiative in the formalization process, because the domain of interest—telephony—is highly constrained and because the programs being specified—call control features—are relatively small. Our work is concerned with larger, less constrained design problems where greater analyst involvement is needed. It is also more aimed toward the construction of specific behaviors starting from more general requirements. Nevertheless, we have recognized for some time that acquisition from scenarios is a useful complement to the work we are doing in highly constrained design situations [22], and Benner in our group is currently investigating this area further [6].

The PRISMA project [30] is also a system for assisting in the construction of specifications from requirements. Its main characteristics are as follows:

1. Multiple views of the (emerging) specification, where the views that they have explored are data-flow diagrams, entity relationship models, and Petri nets.
2. Each view is represented in the same underlying semantic-net formalism yet represents a different aspect of the specification. This representation is suited to graphical presentation and admits to certain consistency and completeness heuristics whose semantics

depend on the view being represented (e.g., the lack of an "input" link in this representation in a data-flow diagram indicates a process lacking inputs; in an entity-relationship diagram it indicates an entity with no attributes; in a Petri net diagram it indicates an event with no preconditions (prior events)).

3. Heuristics exist to compare the different views of (different aspects of) the same specification, and aid in construction of new views or support checking for partial consistency between views.
4. Errors detected by the above heuristics are added to an agenda of tasks requiring resolution, along with advice on how to accomplish that resolution.
5. A paraphraser produces natural-language presentations of many of the kinds of information manipulated by the system (e.g., of the requirements information represented in the different views, of the agenda of tasks and advice for performing those tasks, and of the results of the heuristics that detect uses of requirements freedoms).

There is striking similarity between their approach and ours—the use of multiple views and their presentations, and an underlying semantic-net formalism. They have clearly thought about and developed heuristics to operate on or between views, an aspect that we have only recently begun to address. Conversely, we have provided much more support for evolution.

9. Summary

ARIES provides a variety of capabilities to support the process of requirements acquisition and analysis. These capabilities include acquisition, review, evolution support, analysis, and reuse support. These are intended to help analysts satisfy the conflicting goals of software requirements specification in a gradual and systematic way. The system as a whole focuses on the problems of describing systems from different viewpoints, and reconciling different viewpoints.

By building the ARIES prototype, we have been able to identify and offer solutions for many of the significant challenges that must be met in making knowledge-based requirements and specification development environments a reality. Specifically, we have concentrated on supporting reuse of large domain independent and dependent knowledge-bases, providing multipresentation acquisition along with significant automation support in the form of evolution transformations, specification analysis, and simulations. We have developed mechanisms around many requirements support features including folders, reuse techniques, acquisition and review, analysis and simulation, evolution transformations, and traceability. Work on the project is ongoing; most of the capabilities envisioned for the system are already in place, but much work remains to be done.

Acknowledgments

We wish to thank Kevin Benner for comments on this paper. Charles Rich has provided important guidance to this work. We would like to acknowledge current and previous members of the ARIES project: Jay Myers, K. Narayanaswamy, Jay Runkel, and Lorna Zorman. This work was sponsored in part by the U.S. Air Force Systems Command, Rome Air Development Center, under contracts F30602-85-C-0221 and F30602-89-C-0103. It was also sponsored in part by the U.S. Department of Defense Advanced Research Projects Agency under contract no. NCC-2-520. Views and conclusions contained in this paper are the authors and should not be interpreted as representing the official opinion or policy of the U.S. government or any agency thereof.

Notes

1. ARIES stands for *A*cquisition of *R*equirements and *I*ncremental *E*volution of *S*pecifications.
2. This diagram is reprinted from [4].
3. Refine [32] is a trademark of Reasoning Systems Inc. It is derived from the V language [36].
4. The reader may not that not all relations can be reified, otherwise there would be an infinite regression of representing relations as objects, whose attributes are relations represented as objects, etc. To avoid this problem we distinguish on a case-by-case basis whether relations are to be treated as sets of tuples or as sets of objects. In particular, those relations that represent the fundamental roles in case grammar, e.g., actor, object, etc., are primitive relations implemented as sets of tuples.

References

1. J.S. Anderson and S. Fickas, "A proposed perspective shift: Viewing specification design as a planning problem," in *Proc. 5th Int. Workshop Software Specification and Design*, Pittsburgh, PA, pp. 177–184, Computer Society Press of the IEEE, May 1989.
2. ASA, *Airman's Information Manual*. Aviation Supplies and Academics: Seattle, WA, 1989.
3. R. Balzer, D. Cohen, M.S. Feather, N.M. Goldman, W. Swartout, and D.S. Wile. "Operational specification as the basis for specifiction validation," *Theory and Practice of Software Technology*, pp. 21–49. North-Holland: Amsterdam, 1983.
4. R. Balzer, C. Green, and T. Cheatham. "Software technology in the 1990s using a new paradigm," *IEEE Computer*, vol. 16, no. 11, pp. 39–45, November 1983.
5. K. Benner, "Using simulation techniques to analyze specifications," in *Proc. 5th KBSA Conf.*, Syracuse, NY, pp. 305–316, 1990. Data Analysis Center for Software.
6. K. Benner and W.L. Johnson, "The use of scenarios for the development and validation of specifications," in *Proc. Comput. Aerospace VII Conf.*, Monterey, CA, 1989.
7. A. Borgida, S. Greenspan, and J. Mylopoulos. "Knowledge representation as the basis for requirements specifications," *IEEE Comput.*, vol. 18, no. 4, pp. 82–91, April 1985.
8. R.M. Burstall and J. Goguen. "Putting theories together to make specifications," in *Proc. 5th Int. Conf. Artificial Intell.*, Cambridge, MA, pp. 1045–1058, August 1977.
9. D. Cohen. Symbolic execution of the gist specification language," in *Proc. 8th Int. Joint Conf. Artificial Intell.*, pp. 17–20, IJCAI, Karlsruhe, 1983.
10. D. Cohen. *AP5 Manual*. USC-Information Sciences Institute: Marina del Rey, CA, June 1989. Draft.
11. A.M. Davis. *Software Requirements Analysis and Specification*. Prentice-Hall: Englewood Cliffs, NJ, 1990.
12. M.S. Feather," Constructing specifications by combining parallel elaborations," *IEEE Trans. Software Eng.* vol. 15, no. 2, pp. 198–208, February 1989. Available as research report #RS-88-216 from ISI, 4676 Admiralty Way, Marina del Rey, CA 90292.
13. S. Fickas, "A knowledge-based approach to specification acquisition and construction," Technical Report 86-1, Computer Science Dept., University of Oregon, Eugene, 1986.
14. N.M. Goldman, "Three dimensions of design development," in *Proc. 3rd Nat. Conf. Artificial Intell.*, Washington, DC, pp. 130–133, August 1983.

15. C. Green, D. Luckham, R. Balzer, T. Cheatham, and C. Rich. "Report on a knowledge-based software assistant," *Readings in Artificial Intelligence and Software Engineering*, pp. 377–428, Morgan Kaufmann: Los Altos, CA, 1986.

16. J. Hagelstein, "Declarative approach to information system requirements," *J. Knowledge-Based Syst.*, vol. 1, no. 4, pp. 211–220, September 1988.

17. F.G. Halasz, T.P. Moran, and R.H. Trigg, "Notecards in a nutshell." Technical Report, Xerox PARC, 1986.

18. D. Harel, H. Lachover, A. Naamad, A. Pnueli, M. Politi, R. Sherman, and A. Shtul-Trauring, "Statemate: A working environment for the development of complex reactive systems," in *Proc. 10th Int. Conf. Software Eng.*, Singapore, pp. 396–406, 1988.

19. D. Harris and A. Czuchry, "The knowledge-based requirements assistant," *IEEE Expert*, vol. 3, no. 4, 1988.

20. K.E. Huff and V.R. Lesser, "The GRAPPLE plan formalism," Technical Report 87-08, University of Massachusetts, Department of Computer and Information Science, April 1987.

21. V. Hunt and A. Zellweger, "The FAA's advanced automation system: Strategies for future air traffic control systems," *IEEE Comput.* vol. 20, no. 2, pp. 19–32, February 1987.

22. W.L. Johnson, "Specification via scenarios and views," in *Proc. 3d Int. Software Process Workshop*, Breckenridge, CO, pp. 61–63, 1986.

23. W.L. Johnson, "Deriving specifications from requirements," in *Proc. 10th Int. Conf. Software Eng.*, Singapore, pp. 428–437, 1988.

24. W.L. Johnson, "Specification as formalizing and transforming domain knowledge," in *Proc. AAAI Workshop on Automating Software Design*, St. Paul, MN, pp. 48–55, 1988.

25. W.L. Johnson and M.S. Feather, "Using evolution transformations to construct specifications," *Automating Software Design*. AAAI Press: Cambridge, MA, 1991, in press.

26. W.L. Johnson and K. Yue, "An integrated specification development framework," Technical Report RS-88-215, University of Southern California, Information Sciences Institute, Marina del Rey, CA, 1988.

27. V.E. Kelly and U. Nonnenmann, Reducing the complexity of formal specification acquisition," in *Proc. AAAI-88 Workshop on Automating Software Design*, St. Paul, MN, pp. 66–72, 1988.

28. R. Mac Gregor. *Loom Users Manual*, USC/ISI, Marina del Rey, CA, 1989.

29. J.J. Myers and W.L. Johnson, "Towards specification explanation: Issues and lessons," in *Proc. 3d Knowledge-Based Software Assistant Conf.*, Rome, NY, pp. 251–269, 1988.

30. C. Niskier, T. Maibaum, and D. Schwabe, "A look through PRISMA: Towards pluralistic knowledge-based environments for software specification acquisition, "in *Proc. 5th Int. Workshop on Software Specification and Design*, Pittsburgh, PA, pp. 128–136. Computer Society Press of the IEEE, May 1989.

31. The KBSA Project. Knowledge-based specification assistant: Final report. Unpublished, USC/ISI, Marina del Ray, CA, 1988.

32. *Refine User's Guide*, Reasoning Systems, Palo Alto, CA, 1986.

33. H.B. Rubenstein and R.C. Waters, "The requirements apprentice: An initial scenario," in *Proc. 5th Int. Workshop on Software Specification and Design*, Pittsburgh, PA, May, pp. 211–218. Computer Society Press of the IEEE, 1989.

34. C. Rich, H.E. Schrobe, and R.C. Waters, "An overview of the programmer's apprentice, in *Proc. 6th Int. Joint Conf. Artificial Intell.*, Tokyo, pp. 827–828, 1979.

35. W.N. Robinson, "Integrating multiple specifications using domain goals," in *Proc. 5th Int. Workshop on Software Specification and Design*, Pittsburgh, PA, May, pp. 219–226. Computer Society Press of the IEEE, 1989.

36. D.R. Smith, G.B. Kotik, and S.J. Westfold, "Research on knowledge-based software environments at Kestrel Institute," *IEEE Trans. Software Eng.*, vol. SE-11, no. 11, pp. 1278–1295, 1985.

37. G.L. Steele, Jr., "The definition and implementation of a computer programming language," Technical Report 595, MIT Artificial Intelligence Laboratory, Cambridge, MA 1980.

38. W. Swartout, "Gist English generator," in *Proc. Nat. Conf. Artificial Intell.*, Pittsburgh, PA, pp. 404–409, AAAI, 1982.

39. R.C. Waters, "The programmer's apprentice: A session with KBEmacs," *IEEE Trans. Software Eng.*, vol. SE-11, no. 11, pp. 1296–1320, November 1985.

Journal of Systems Integration, 1, 321–337 (1991)
© 1991 Kluwer Academic Publishers, Boston. Manufactured in The Netherlands.

CASE Planning and the Software Process[1]

WATTS S. HUMPHREY

Software Engineering Institute,[2] Carnegie-Mellon University, Pittsburgh, PA 15213

(Received January 15, 1990; Revised March 27, 1990)

Abstract. Automating a software process magnifies its strengths and accentuates its weaknesses. Automation can make an effective process more effective, but it can also make a chaotic process even worse—and at considerable expense. Anyone who buys expensive tools to solve an ill-defined problem is likely to be disappointed. Unless such tools are obtained as part of a thoughtful software process improvement plan, the purchase could be an expensive mistake. This article discusses software process maturity and its relationship to planning and installing computer-aided software engineering (CASE) systems. Although process is not a magic answer (there isn't one), the key issues are discussed from a process perspective, and guidelines are given for avoiding the most common pitfalls. Because CASE systems can involve significant investment, an economic justification may be necessary. The relevant financial considerations are therefore discussed, and some basic steps for producing such justifications are outlined. Finally, some key considerations for introducing and using CASE systems are discussed.

Key Words: case, process, planning, management, improvement, software, process maturity model, economic justification, software teams

1. Introduction

In discussing computer-aided software engineering (CASE), it is important to first define what we mean by the software process and its relationship to creativity, methodology, and automation. As used here, the software process is the set of activities, methods, and practices that guide people in the production of software. An effective process must consider the required tasks, the tools and methods, and the software developers' skills, training, and motivation. Because many people have trouble visualizing the concept of process as applied to software development, an analogy to a manufacturing operation can be helpful. A factory is more than just a collection of tools; it includes, e.g., work flow control, incoming material handling, inventory control, measurement and monitoring, quality control systems, and emergency procedures. Although software development is more varied and knowledge intensive than is traditional manufacturing, it also has a great deal of routine. Unfortunately, it is the poor handling of this routine that causes many of software's manageability problems. Typical examples of such routine are change control, error tracking, configuration management, and cost estimation.

[1]This material is based in part on material from, Watts S. Humphrey, *Managing the Software Process*, Addison-Wesley, Reading, MA, © 1989. Reprinted with permission.
[2]This work was sponsored by the U.S. Department of Defense. The ideas and findings in this report should not be construed as an official DoD position. It is published in the interest of scientific and technical information exchange.

Several reasons for defining the software process are to:

1. Clearly identify the roles of the involved people and organizations.
2. Identify the routine tasks.
3. Provide common direction for executing these routine tasks, possibly through procedures or automation.
4. Free the professionals from time-consuming routine and permit them to devote more energy to creative tasks.
5. Provide a mechanism for continuously incorporating process improvements.

Although the need to control or eliminate routine through procedure or automation is obvious, the role of methodology is not as clear. The effective performance of complex tasks requires a clear understanding of human limitations. Because people can only comprehend limited amounts of detail, the common approach to complexity has been to establish hierarchies of abstractions to represent various levels of detail. In large-scale data processing systems, for example, we think of the programs in several parts: the operating system, file management, network management, and applications, for example. As appropriate, each of these can be further subdivided.

This, essentially, is a notational system where we generate symbols to represent complex entities. Because it seems so obvious, it is easy to miss the significance of notation. For example, Roman numerals were generally used in the Western world up until about 1400 A.D. It took 800 years for the superior Hindu–Arabic system to reach general use, but this notation has enabled us to think in far richer terms than would otherwise be possible. For another example, try, in your head, to multiply the binary numbers 1100101 and 1010111. In decimal notation the answer is trivial: $101 \times 87 = 8787$.

In software, the role of method is to provide powerful notations and rules for using them. This identifies a crucial reason for CASE systems: to facilitate a methodology. That is, CASE can provide a convenient way to define and manipulate the symbols defined by the methodology. This implies two levels of operation: symbol manipulation at the current level of concentration and symbol decomposition through all the relevant levels of the notational hierarchy.

The basic reason for using CASE systems to automate the software process is to improve the quality and productivity of the work. By reducing tasks to routine procedures and mechanizing them labor is saved and sources of human error are eliminated. The latter, it turns out, is the most effective way to improve productivity: greater software productivity improvements come from eliminating mistakes than from performing tasks more efficiently [1]. Although better tools and procedures cannot replace creative designers, poor ones can frustrate and impede them.

To do a consistently effective job on a complex task, it is necessary to consciously understand what is being done. Although some people are so talented that they unconsciously do superb work, an intuitive process is more risky with larger tasks and multiperson teams. A more orderly focus on process definition and improvement is then advisable.

For a complex process to be understood, it must be relatively stable and not subject to wild fluctuation. W. Edwards Deming, who inspired the postware Japanese industrial miracle, refers to this as statistical control [2]. When a process is under statistical control, repeating the work in roughly the same way will produce roughly the same result. Then, to get consistently better results, we must improve the process. Sustained improvement is possible only if the process is under statistical control. Thus, the first management challenge is to make the software process reasonably stable and effective. As Stenning says, "the role of an environment is to support effective use of an effective process [3]." After the process has become stable and is reasonably effective, we can consider automation to improve its efficiency. It is, of course, always helpful to use better notations and methods.

Before proceeding further, it is necessary to define what CASE means. One published definition says that "computer-aided software engineering (CASE) is the application of automated technologies to the software engineering procedures" [4]. This definition encompasses the entire range from individual task-oriented tools to fully integrated operational software environments. This article addresses the latter: planning and installing a comprehensive software environment. Such an environment should be based on a sound methodology and include a set of compatible tools, a common database, task management facilities, and provisions for configuration control. When the term "CASE system" is used in this article, it refers to this type of comprehensive support environment.

Although some CASE systems presume design and implementation methodologies, others provide more flexibility—and consequently less guidance in the way the work is to be done. As CASE systems become more sophisticated, their notations and procedures are necessarily more closely involved with the practitioners' personal working practices. As a result, common disciplines and methods become necessary, along with common procedures, conventions, standards, interfaces, and measures. For example, complications arise unless a project selects a common implementation language or agrees on a single configuration management system. Less obviously needed are such things as common notations, design methods, and integration procedures. If an organization has not already established such a common working framework, the installation of a CASE system can be traumatic. Even though a common framework is a key aspect of a mature software process, the sudden imposition of such constraints could easily seem to result from the CASE system itself. Such apparent sharp reductions in the freedom and flexibility of the working professionals can cause resentment and resistance unless the system is carefully planned and introduced.

This article also discusses CASE systems in a somewhat idealized sense. Although their ultimate full range of capabilities is not yet entirely clear, it is likely that CASE systems will evolve in much the same way as many of the other system facilities common to software. A large-scale database system, for example, provides a basic framework and a set of utilities. In deciding how to use these capabilities, the users must define the data types, the precise data formats and relationships, the desired outputs and their formats, and the operational and control procedures. The design of the database system imposes constraints on many of these decisions, but users generally have considerable flexibility in their precise use.

In the comprehensive CASE systems of the future, the situation should be similar: a wide range of basic capabilities will be provided, but the users will have to select the systems that most closely meet their needs and then tailor the protocols, formats, procedures, and methods to their specific tasks. For relatively standardized uses, it is also likely that sets of "canned" facilities will be provided so that less demanding users could accept these built-in choices rather than tailor their own. This approach, however, also poses a serious danger: the standardized CASE system facilities may not fit the user's intended need. This is why, at least at this early stage in CASE systems development, inexperienced users must be doubly careful. They should first determine the classes of methods that will best fit their needs and only then select a CASE system that supports such methods.

2. Software Process Maturity

In early 1987, the Software Engineering Institute (SEI) at Carnegie-Mellon University in Pittsburgh, PA, launched a program to specialize in the software process. The objective was to help software organizations to improve their software capabilities. This focus on software process was based on the premises that the process of producing and evolving software products can be defined, managed, measured, and progressively improved and that the quality of a software product is largely governed by the quality of the process used to create, repair, and improve it.

Successful software work requires capable and motivated technical people, knowledge of the ultimate application environment, and detailed understanding of the end user's needs [5]. These factors alone, however, are not enough: the key missing ingredient, generally, is effective software process management. Software process management is the application of process engineering concepts, techniques, and practices to monitor, control, and improve the software process. As software organizations grow larger and their projects become more complex, process management becomes progressively more important. In fact, the lack of effective process management causes many otherwise capable software groups to be ineffective.

To address software process issues, the SEI developed a process maturity model and a related software process assessment instrument [6]. These are the basic elements of the SEI method for examining and improving the software process [7]. By using these elements, an organization's software engineering capability can be characterized with the aid of the software process maturity model. Organizations can then determine the priority actions required for improving their software capability.

As shown in Figure 1, this model consists of five maturity levels and the key activities required at each level. These maturity levels have been selected because they reasonably represent the historical improvement phases of actual software organizations, represent a measure of improvement that can realistically be achieved from the prior level, suggest interim improvement goals and progress measures, and make obvious a set of immediate improvement priorities once an organization's status in this framework is known.

At the initial level (level 1), an organization can be characterized as having an ad hoc, or possibly chaotic, process. Typically, the organization operates without formalized procedures, cost estimates, or project plans. Even if formal project control procedures exist, there are inadequate management mechanisms to ensure they are followed. Tools are not well integrated with the process, nor are they uniformly applied. Change control is rarely adequate, and senior management is not exposed to or does not understand the key software problems and issues. When projects do succeed, it is generally due to the heroic efforts of a dedicated team rather than the capability of the organization.

An organization at the repeatable level (level 2) has established basic project controls: project planning, management oversight, software quality assurance, and change control.

Maturity Level/Key Issues

Level	Characteristic	Key Problem Areas	Result
5 Optimizing	Improvement fed back into process	Automation	**Productivity & Quality**
4 Managed	(quantitative) Measured process	Changing technology Problem analysis Problem prevention	
3 Defined	(qualitative) Process defined and institutionalized	Process measurement Process analysis Quantitative quality plans	
2 Repeatable	(intuitive) Process dependent on individuals	Training Technical practices • reviews, testing Process focus • standards, process groups	
1 Initial	(ad hoc / chaotic)	Project management Project planning Configuration management Software quality assurance	**Risk**

Figure 1. Software process maturity model.

The strength of the organization stems from its experience at doing the same kind of work many times, and it generally does reasonably well at meeting its schedule and cost commitments. Such organizations, however, face major risks when presented with new challenges. They also have frequent quality problems and generally lack an orderly framework for process improvement.

At the defined level (level 3), the organization has laid the foundation for examining the process and deciding how to improve it. The keys to moving from the repeatable level to the defined level are to establish a software engineering process group (SEPG), establish a software process architecture that defines the key process activities, review the adequacy of the training program, and introduce a family of software engineering methods and technologies. Although all these issues could usefully be addressed at level 2 or even at level 1, special focus on them is required at this point to permit further progress to level 4.

The managed level (level 4) builds on the foundation established at the defined level. When the process is defined, it can be examined and improved, but there is little data to measure effectiveness. Thus, to advance to the managed level, an organization needs to establish a minimum set of measurements for the quality and productivity parameters of each key task. The organizaion also needs a process database with resources to manage and maintain it, analyze the data, and advise project members on its meaning and use. These data are useful not only for managing the process but also for justifying the necessary investments in training, staffing, and CASE systems.

Two requirements are fundamental to advance from the managed to the optimizing level (level 5): data gathering should be automated, and management should give highest priority to process analysis and improvement. At the optimizing level, the organization has the means

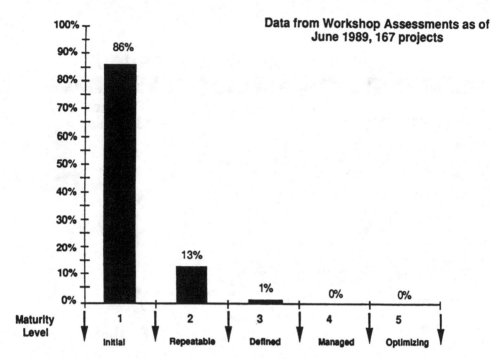

Figure 2. Software process maturity distribution.

to identify the weakest process elements and strenghten them; data are available to justify applying technology to the most critical tasks; and numerical evidence is available on process effectiveness. The key additional activities at the optimizing level are rigorous defect cause analysis and defect prevention. When each key task is completed, the people who were involved conduct a brief postmortem to determine what went wrong, what should be fixed, and what could be improved. This provides the organization with the essential data for making process improvements. These activities are important because they provide a routine mechanism for maintaining continuous focus on process improvement. Although there are many aspects to the transition form one maturity level to another, the basic objective is to achieve a controlled and measured process as the foundation for continued improvement.

This maturity framework has been used as the basis for an assessment program conducted by the SEI to determine the state of the software process in United States software organizations. As shown in Figure 2, early indications are that currently approximately 84% of U.S. software organizations are at level 1, and only about 14% are at level 2 [8]. It is thus likely that most organizations considering the installation of CASE systems will be at level 1, the least-mature level of software process management. Before addressing the key issues these organizations are likely to face, the reasons for automating the software process are discussed next.

3. Why CASE Is Needed

At present, software development is a human-intensive process with all the limitations that implies. For example, people can do things only so fast. We accept the four-minute mile as near the limit of human capability and see the three-minute mile as beyond human aspiration. Human intellectual capabilities are also limited. Airline pilots, for example, can only focus on a limited number of actions at once and their performance degrades with fatigue. There are similar limits to the quality and production of software developers, but they are not as clear. Although human capabilities do seem to improve with time, these improvements are only gradual. Clearly, to make major improvement, our hopes must increasingly rest on some new conceptual view of our tasks or the use of more powerful tools.

Although we can and should continue the search for better concepts and methods, consistent and sustained software process improvements must ultimately come from technology. Improved tools and methods have been helpful throughout the history of software; but once the software process reaches level 5 maturity (optimizing), we will be in a far better position to understand where and how technology can help.

In advancing from the level 1 (chaotic) process, we can make major improvements by simply turning a crowd of programmers into a coordinated team of professionals. Perlis put it best in 1968 when he said, "We kid ourselves if we believe that software systems can only be designed and built by a small number of people. If we adopt that view this subject will remain precisely as it is today, and will ultimately die. We must learn how to build software systems with hundreds, possibly thousands of people [9]." This is the challenge faced by immature software organizations: how to plan and coordinate the creative work of their professionals so they support rather than interfere with each other.

Software process management addresses this need by providing a framework for progressively improving the orderliness of the work. By moving from the initial (level 1) to the repeatable (level 2) and then to the defined (level 3) process, the commitment framework is established to coordinate large operations. By using a structured, managed, and planned process, the professionals better understand their roles and their interrelationships. The defined software process then facilitates more rational reactions to the surprises and challenges of the work.

Once orderly performance is achieved, improvement continues but only in increments. At some point, the professionals are using the process about as effectively as they can; yet further quality and productivity improvements will still be needed. At this point, what additional steps can be taken, and what limitations will ultimately be met?

Although there are many opportunities for improving software technology, there is also the potential for significantly improving software process support. By making tools more consistent and integrating them in a common CASE system, it will be possible to move beyond task support to support of the full life cycle. The need here, for example, is for common user interfaces, facilitywide data models, and coherent intermediate languages and formats. As CASE systems grow more sophisticated, their ability to support common understanding of management and technical plans will improve as will their ability to guide the execution of individual tasks so they better relate to the total job. Any large software project uses a complex process, and it is often difficult to know which steps are most appropriate at any point. For example, after a system test, should one merely fix the problems and ship or would some redesign, reinspection, or retest be appropriate? And, if so, for what parts of the system? Data gathering and analysis also require support to be more accurate, timely, and economical. Although automated support for these activities will come only gradually, organizations should take early steps to develop a software process support strategy. When this strategy is coupled with a concerted effort to improve process maturity to level 3 or better, the organization will have a sound framework for orderly and steady improvement and a realistic basis for CASE installation.

4. CASE Planning Guidelines

Although it is risky to propose universal guidelines at this early stage in CASE technology development, the following five appear to be generally applicable. Clearly, with further experience, a great deal more will be learned. Although these CASE-planning guidelines should be reasonably durable, they are based on limited experience. They must, therefore, be reexamined as new data become available.

4.1. Guideline 1: If Your Process is Chaotic, Get It Under Control Before Attempting to Install a CASE System

A level 1 organization's first priority is to reach level 2 by getting its software process under control before it attempts to install a sophisticated CASE system. To be fully effective, CASE systems must envorce a common set of policies, procedures, and methods on their users. If the systems are used with an immature process, the environment will merely become another bureaucracy, only an unavoidable one. The saving grace of most immature organizations is that their poor management system permits their ineffective process to be circumvented by their professionals. The truly unworkable steps have been skillfully evaded thus permitting the professionals to produce in spite of the system. When a CASE system enforces an unworkable process, it generally brings the level 1 organization to its knees.

It is possible to use CASE systems as collections of individual tools. Although this is an expensive way to obtain compilers and editors, it can be a reasonable step toward standardizing on a single tool set in preparation for later support improvements. For any more sophisticated use, however, the most important single rule is: if the process is chaotic, get it under control before attempting to install a CASE system. Many groups have brought their process under control by following a well-defined improvement program [1]. The basic steps required are briefly summarized in the conclusion of this article.

4.2. Guideline 2: Develop Your Process Before or During CASE Installation but Not After

Many organizations that work with CASE systems have barely reached level 2 or are struggling to get there. Thus, they have not made much progress in defining their process. The first task such groups generally formalize is configuration management, and some groups may even establish strong procedures for requirements validation and change. These are appropriate processes to consider for initial trial implementation with a CASE system.

Beyond this, the organization should establish a full-time group of experienced software development professionals to work on process improvement. This group should either include or work closely with the technology group responsible for planning and supporting CASE implementation. These two groups, the software engineering process group (SEPG) and the CASE support group, then form the core for continued software process development and automation. If such dedicated groups are not established, there is usually no one who is consistently attending to the problems of process control and improvement. Based on studies of a large number of software organizations, such groups typically remain at the level 1 of process maturity [8]. Under these conditions, the process will generally stagnate and the CASE system will cease to evolve in step with the organization's needs and capabilities. When no one is assigned to work on process development, improvement is unlikely—after all, the process cannot improve itself.

4.3. Guideline 3: System Conversion Is Critical, but Converting the People Will Be the Hardest Job of All

In the broadest sense, conversion to a new support environment involves far more than the obtaining and installing the hardware and software. Often, a more challenging job is that of converting all the software that is being actively developed and maintained. Here, care is required to ensure that version control is not compromised and that provisions are made to move all the ongoing work to the new environment.

Although these tasks are often challenging, the "people issues" are generally even more complex. The management of change, in fact, is itself a well-defined process as well [10]. When done properly, management of change helps the people accept the need for the proposed change, convinces them that the selected CASE system is a proper choice, and helps them prepare for the transition. It is also essential that workers be supported by specialists in the systems and procedures they will be using.

Of all the many facets to the "people issue," adequately training on how to convert to and use the new facilities is most important. In fact, training is the most common single weakness of level 2 organizations. Professional programmers often will not accept, and may not even be able to use, advanced tools effectively unless they are adequately trained. Training is also very expensive, and most organizations have many different groups that each have their unique training needs. In one organization, just the tool training costs for a 30-person programming shop came to $162,000, and this did not include the required instructional hardware and software. In another case, per-tool training costs were projected as $1507 per person, so each professional's training for a simple six-tool CASE system cost $9042 [11]. Beyond this, training in languages, design methods, inspections, and testing is often needed, to name just a jew of the topics. Training is likely to be very expensive but not nearly as expensive as not training.

4.4. Guideline 4: Recognize that a CASE Installation Is Never Completed

The people, their experience level, the available technology, process methods, the business environment, and project needs all change with time. The environmental support system must thus also change and evolve. Although it is essential to maintain reasonable environmental stability, people's capabilities change and new problems arise that require attention.

It is therefore essential to maintain continuing resources to plan, support, and control CASE evolution. This requires a permanent staff, a system for reporting and tracking problems, mechanisms to periodically assess the users' needs, and the capability to test and prototype changes before putting them into general use.

As pointed out in guideline 2, a CASE support group is needed to provide assistance, interface with the vendors, and lead the CASE planning and installation efforts. These tasks, however, require a delicate balance between the roles of champion, advocate, and manager. The champion sells the organization on the need for CASE. The advocate understands the organization's needs and represents them to the vendors. The manager develops the plans, musters the resources, and directs the implementation. All this, of course, implies an orderly, planned approach. That is another reason for guideline 1: if the organization's software process is chaotic, its CASE planning and installation efforts will likely be chaotic as well.

4.5. Guideline 5: Don't Forget to Think!

With inappropriate automation, it is easy to induce online frenzy, abstraction distraction, or object hypnosis. The introduction of powerful tools carries the risk of damage through misuse. For example, powerful tools make mindless action so easy that enormous heaps of code can be produced without much thought. Although it is generally possible to use a CASE system as an aid to a manual architectural design, both managers and implementors get impatient waiting for design completion and may prematurely rush into implementation. When the environment's powerful facilities have been oversold, management may believe it is capable of far more than it can possibly provide. Good designs start with functional and structural concepts, and no machine can produce these. When the developers rapidly produce mountains of detail, it is easy to believe that the environment has provided an orderly framework. Without clear concepts, this frenzied rush to implement can easily produce abstraction nestings with dozens of levels or case statements with thousands of choices. When such absurdities pervade a system, it can become irreparable even with the best available tools.

The basic guideline is to select your design methods with care and not just because they came with the tool; then insist on a thorough high-level architectural design to establish the system structure, define the system components, and specify and control their interfaces. This will establish a solid foundation for everything that follows.

5. Planning and Installing CASE Systems

Although a full treatment of CASE planning and installation is beyond the scope of this article, a few general considerations are worth special attention. First, and most important, it is essential to have senior management support. By starting with their agreement on the need for a comprehensive plan, it is easier to establish success criteria and obtain needed financial, administrative, and technical support. Before proceeding too far, it is wise to review with the sponsoring executives the study plan, decision criteria, required support, and any identified issues.

Next, just as with a product effort, it is advisable to start with a comprehensive study of CASE requirements. The resulting document should clearly state management's objectives for the system and its critical functions. These functions should be prioritized, however, or they will likely become so voluminous as to provide little guidance. After all, if everything is needed, and not all desired functions can be provided at once, the crucial task of setting priorities is left to the implementors.

One approach is to establish three priorities: (1) essential for the first installation, (2) required as an early enhancement, and (3) desirable in the future. It is then wise to get both technical and project management agreement with these priorities. As the planning becomes more specific, installation and conversion commitments will be facilitated if priorities 1, 2, and 3 are known for each key project. If no project is willing to convert to and use the CASE system at an early date, the plan should be reevaluated and the priority 1 items reestablished.

Over time, comprehensive CASE systems are likely to be the single most expensive capital investment a software organization makes. Although it is not clear what such systems will cost, ultimately CASE system acquisition and support costs could easily exceed those of the organization's other software, computing systems, and terminals combined. Most software professionals can, with modest effort, get approval to purchase a software package for a few hundred dollars. When the costs mount to a few thousand dollars, a manager's approval is generally required. When the costs rise much beyond this, hard data will be required. The question then becomes: what data is necessary and how can it be presented to win approval?

5.1. Developing the Economic Justification

Although any reasonably conducted financial study will likely produce the required results, substantial work is generally required. The following steps are not proposed as the only or even the best way to produce such a justification; they have, however, been used with some success.

1. Install and evaluate some limited prototypes to validate vendor claims and obtain preliminary usage data.
2. Develop a task map for the technology currently in use and another task map for the task that is planned.
3. Identify the current resource expenditure profiles for each task. These numbers must be reviewed and accepted by the managers of the most critical projects.
4. Assemble a team of experts to determine the resource impact of the new CASE system and its associated support tools and methods. This team should also consider the likely quality consequences at each process stage and should use the same level of detail as the task maps. When completed, this information is also reviewed with the project managers and their leading technical people.
5. Review each project's migration plan to determine the accrual rate of the savings. Do not forget to include a learning curve as well as the anticipated product quality benefits in the test, installation, and repair phases.

6. Get each project's commitment to this savings schedule, together with agreement to adjust project plans accordingly. This will not be easy, but it is the only way to convince the finance people that this investment is worthwhile.
7. Establish a new schedule of estimating factors for project planning.
8. Estimate the planning, training, installation, conversion, and support costs.
9. Construct a composite savings schedule for the organization as a whole. If the information is available, reference to other organizations' experiences can add considerable credibility.
10. Get competent financial advice on the methods used and the results anticipated.
11. With this justification, request management approval for the plan.

Although most of these steps are relatively straightforward, the task map in step 2 is not. Essentially, it consists of a structured picture of the software process with identification of each key task and the tools and methods used in performing it. The work is analyzed in sufficient detail to identify the specific costs associated with each of these key tasks and to determine the anticipated costs with the new CASE system. Because some of the most significant savings are likely to result from improved quality and the resulting reduced testing and repair costs, it is also essential to estimate the improved quality consequences for each process task. A carefully conducted prototype evaluation in step 1 should provide a basis for much of this work. The development of an economic justification is impossible without the support of project managers. Even with their support, it will be hard to sell cost-conscious senior management on a major investment that does not directly increase revenue. With enough support and persistence, however, the case can be made.

5.2. Economic Justification—Special Considerations

In generating an economic justification, it is helpful to keep these special considerations in mind:

1. Level 1 organizations do not have the data to make an economic justification. Level 2 organizations generally have to make an extensive study to produce a rudimentary justification. Level 3 groups have the cost data but need to conduct a special study to estimate the quality factors. Level 4 and 5 groups have the needed data readily at hand.
2. In projecting savings, do not get too far out on a technological limb; focus on practical and achievable improvements.
3. Involve the financial people. A professionally prepared financial story takes a lot of work, but it will be far more convincing to the intended audience than a technical presentation.
4. Do the work in detail. Although the detail will not be presented, bring a well-structured summary of the results as backup. It is rarely needed, but a thick pile of backup material builds the presenter's confidence and deters the most detail-minded financial executive.
5. Approval is unlikely without line management's agreement and savings commitments from the project mangers.
6. Remember that there is no way to absolutely prove the economic value of a CASE system. This, however, is generally true of any other capital investment. Although this is not

a useful arguing point, it is worth remembering during the financial debates. When the executives are convinced of the soundness of the study and recommendations, they will not require absolute proof.

Although some people have reported dramatic early savings from CASE systems, others have reported that a fully automated CASE system, by enforcing a comprehensive design discipline, actually increased early costs [12]. If initial expectations were too high, the CASE system could be blamed for such startup costs and the entire effort jeopardized. Since such cost increases generally result from more complete early design work, later benefits in reduced testing and improved product quality could easily pay for the entire CASE installation.

The early costs are also likely to be inflated by the added time required for the professionals to become familiar with the new system and the procedures and methods it entails. This learning curve should be tracked with the early installations so that subsequent users can be better informed when making their plans.

5.3. Installing CASE Systems

If the planning has been done properly and adequate training and support facilities are available, the actual installation and conversion to a CASE system should be relatively straightforward. This does not mean that this phase is easy, however, because any change in the working fabric of an organization is a major upheaval, and many surprises and problems will invariably occur. With adequate preparation, these problems can generally be handled.

One possible exception is an attempt to convert an existing project to a new CASE system. This is always difficult, but it should not even be attempted unless the project is at or very near level 2. Such projects generally have large staffs and major investments in existing designs, test suites, and code. Users should, therefore, treat claims for improved quality and productivity with some skepticism and carefully balance the promised benefits against the more certain costs and risks of a change. On the other hand, if the project is near the beginning of a long development program or is early in its maintenance phase, there may be sufficient reason for a change. The long-term benefits of improved tracking, better design disciplines, and comprehensive change control are often sufficiently attractive to warrant conversion. The key rule, however, is to always keep one foot on solid ground. This requires extended dual system operation and successful performance in slave mode before the first trial cutover. This approach can be very expensive and, in some cases, may not even be feasible. The costs of unanticipated failure are so significant, however, that any precipitous cutover would be foolhardy. Again, such moves should be attempted only if the organization is at or very near level 2.

6. Designing with CASE

Perhaps the most important design consideration with CASE systems is that so little is different: the old familiar design principles are still essential. Although the combination of an effective process and a powerful CASE system can be enormously helpful, when the requirements are wrong, when the application is not understood, or when the conceptual design is ill founded, product results are invariably poor. Although a well-defined and managed process can help identify these problems, it cannot prevent them.

A mature software development process can and should ensure that the proper time and resources are devoted to requirements development, that application needs are thoroughly studied, and that adequate design resources are invested early in the project. It can also ensure a competent expert review of the design itself. When management then attends to the identified concerns, a sound foundation for product development will likely result. Under these conditions, an automated environment can be of greatest value.

With a less mature process, requirements resolution is typically ad hoc; little conscious attention is paid to the design; and there is little provision for expert technical review. Often, customer participation in some technically superficial design review is taken as sufficient evidence that this early work has been done and that code production can begin. Often the result is either a poorly designed product or an expensive and time-consuming remedial design effort during test.

These problems are not generally greatly affected by the introduction of CASE sytems; but the lack of a coherent and well-thought-out conceptual design can cause special problems. Here, the combination of an immature process and an automated environment can create a false sense of security. The CASE system depends on the product's structural design for the partitioning of work between the subsystems, components, and modules. When this system structure lacks coherence, the entire project organization and its support system will be similarly flawed. If this problem is recognized in time and a remedial design effort is launched, the CASE system can greatly assist in the recovery. More often, however, these problems are not recognized until product integration; and then it is hard to stop and rethink the design. More often, management will push ahead and try to patch the problems as they arise. Although this may produce something that actually works, the underlying structural flaws will likely result in a system that is difficult to integrate, impossibly slow, difficult to use, and a maintenance nightmare.

The problems of an incoherent design are always severe, and a CASE system can make them worse. The apparently orderly work flow and the quiet efficiency of change management and status reporting lull the management into believing the product really is well structured. This confusion of efficient method with sound concept can have painful consequences. Designs may have multilayered abstractions with a dozen or more levels or an amoebalike sea of functional objects with no coherent relationships. When such problems pervade the fabric of a system, performance degradations of 1000 times or more are likely, and the resulting kludge may be more expensive to fix than scrapping the design and starting over.

6.1. People Considerations with CASE

Process maturity can be viewed as an evolution in the way people work. Organizations at level 1 typically consist of a largely uncoordinated collection of individuals. Although they may occasionally work together cooperatively, this is more incidental than a result of organization or process. At level 2, collections of small professional teams may work well as single groups, but they do not generally coordinate effectively, except on a largely personal basis. Finally, at level 3 and above, are larger-scale organizational frameworks within which many teams cooperatively interact and support each other. Process maturity is thus not just a management issue but one of establishing the human environment for a large-scale cooperative endeavor.

Perhaps the greatest single people issue with CASE is the need to build a common working ethic and practice. It takes work to build close-knit teams, and many software people object to standard procedures. Enabling a crowd of individual programmers to become a coherent team is a key result of moving from maturity level 1 to level 2. This evolution is a prerequisite to the adoption of the common methods and tools of a CASE system. In spite of the most elaborate preparation, if the professionals are not ready to accept the CASE system as a common working framework, they will treat it as another constraint to be evaded. They have painfully learned to publicly accept imposed policies and procedures and then do whatever is needed to get the job done. This is rarely in accord with the official process. Without a thoughtful program to win the professionals' allegiance, a CASE system installation can then be an expensive blunder.

The current vague or largely nonexistent process definitions typical of most software organizations give the professionals considerable freedom. Stenning points out that "most of the processes used in the software industry would be completely unworkable were it not for human ingenuity and flexibility [3]." In implementing CASE systems, it is essential to recognize that no one is smart enough to define every precise detail of even relatively small parts of the software process. It is thus important that the constraints and controls always leave room for exceptions and escapes. Strong facilities are needed for such items as protection, recovery, change authorization, and promotion control; but even these will need management-authorized escapes. Within these fundamental constraints, the system should permit wide latitude on what tasks are performed, when, and how. As process maturity improves, the professionals better understand how each task should be performed and are better able to judge when and why to use alternatives or exceptions.

6.2. Software Teams and CASE

When a small, coherent team embraces a common process and the CASE system that supports it, powerful results can be expected. When the team retains its structure and has control over its pace for adopting new practices, it will likely remain cohesive even through the installation of a new support system. Such teams are most likely to make a successful CASE installation. An important reason for their success is that the CASE system installation reinforces the team's own efforts to define and improve their working process. We readily accept a football team's need to plan and practice its plays, but somehow the similar needs of programming teams are not recognized. By making this work part of the CASE system migration effort, it becomes more acceptable. Such process work can actually improve a team's performance without the installation or use of a single tool. By ensuring that the entire team fully understands the methods that each member has found most effective, the performance of most teams will improve significantly.

6.3. The CASE Bureaucracy

Even though it will not be apparent until some time after a CASE system has been installed, there is an interesting converse to the acceptance problem. Over time, some professionals will even believe that the CASE system can do no wrong. They will then accept what it produces and blindly follow the steps and actions it prescribes. At that point, the CASE system will have become another and more pervasive bureaucracy that can block rational thought. Although the operation may seem more efficient, its procedures and methods will gradually become less pertinent to current problems. The resulting petrified process can then actually retard organizational improvement. Actions must be taken to ensure that the professionals continue to "own" their own software process, or they will not evolve it in concert with their needs and capabilities. This, of course, is the role of the level 5 optimizing process: it provides the people with a mechanism to review and modify the process in accordance with their current needs.

7. Conclusion

CASE systems hold enormous potential if properly used, but they can also be costly mistakes. When such systems are installed to solve vague and ill-defined problems, they can be a serious disappointment and may even cause harm. After an organization has its software process under control, however, it should certainly investigate CASE systems.

Once the decision is made to proceed with CASE planning and installation, the following initial steps are suggested [1]:

1. Assess the organization. Conduct an orderly study, determine the key problems, and initiate appropriate improvement actions.
2. Establish a software engineering process group (SEPG) to focus on and lead process improvement. If no one is working on process development, improvement is unlikely, for the process can't improve itself.
3. Establish a CASE support group. This responsibility should be assigned to someone who is part of or closely associated with the SEPG and is capable of leading the CASE planning and implementation work. Although such an assignment may not be needed immediately, it will be appropriate as soon as the organization approaches process maturity level 2; and it is absolutely essential to initiating work on installing a CASE system.
4. Plan, manage, and track process improvement with the same discipline used to plan, manage, and track the projects.

Acknowledgments

I am particularly indebted to Brett Bachman, Grady Booch, Anita Carleton, Ken Dymond, Peter Feiler, Louise Hawthorne, Bob Kirkpatrick, Dave Kitson, Steve Masters, Peter Ng, Don O'Neil, Mark Paulk, Ron Radice, Tom Rappath, and Cindy Wise for their helpful comments and suggestions. Linda Pesante has provided very professional editorial assistance, and Dorothy Josephson has, as usual, been invaluable during manuscript preparation; I am also most grateful to both of them for their help. Any errors, omissions, or misstatements are, of course, entirely my responsibility.

References

1. W.S. Humphrey, *Managing the Software Process*. Addison-Wesley: Reading, MA, 1989.
2. W.E. Deming, *Out of the Crisis*. Cambridge, MA: MIT Center of Advanced Engineering Study, 1982.
3. V. Stenning, "On the role of an environment," in *Proc. 9th Int. Conf. Software Eng.*, Monterey, CA, March 30, 1987.
4. A.F. Case, Jr., *Information Systems Development: Principles of Computer-Aided Software Engineering*. Prentice-Hall: Englewood Cliffs, NJ, 1986.
5. B. Curtis, H. Krasner, and N. Iscoe, "A field study of the software design process for large systems," *Commun. ACM* vol. x, no. 2, pp. 00–00, November 1988.
6. W.S. Humphrey, and W.L. Sweet, "A method for assessing the software engineering capability of contractors," SEI Technical Report CMU/SEI-87-TR-23, DTIC: ADA 187230, September 1987.
7. W.S. Humphrey, and D.H. Kitson, "Preliminary report on conducting SEI-assisted assessments of software engineering capability," SEI Technical Report CMU/SEI-87-TR-16, DTIC: ADA 183429, July 1987.
8. W.S. Humphrey, D.H. Kitson, and T.C. Kasse, "The state of software engineering practice: A preliminary report," SEI Technical Report CMU/SEI-89-TR-1, DTIC: ADA 206573, February 1989.
9. P. Naur, and B. Randell, "Software engineering," NATO Science Committee, report, October 1968.
10. W.S. Humphrey, *Managing for Innovation, Leading Technical People*. Prentice-Hall: Englewood Cliffs, NJ, 1987.
11. A. Hughes, "The care and fielding of a software development environment," *Transferring Software Engineering Tool Technology*, S. Przybylinski and P.J. Fowler, Eds., IEEE Computer Society Press, November 1987.
12. P. Lempp, "Productivity and quality gains reported by users of EPOS the integrated CASE environment," *Electro/88 Conf. Rec.*, Boston, MA, May 10–12, 1988.

Journal of Systems Integration, 1, 339–365 (1991)
© 1991 Kluwer Academic Publishers, Boston. Manufactured in The Netherlands.

PProto: An Environment for Prototyping Parallel Programs

RAMÓN D. ACOSTA

International Software Systems, Inc., 9430 Research Blvd., Bldg. 4, #250, Austin, TX 78759

(Received August 22, 1990, Revised May 20, 1991)

Abstract. This paper describes Parallel Proto (PProto), an integrated environment for constructing prototypes of parallel programs. Using functional and performance modeling of dataflow specifications, PProto assists in analysis of high-level software and hardware architectural tradeoffs. Facilities provided by PProto include a visual language and an editor for describing hierarchical dataflow graphs, a resource modeling tool for creating parallel architectures, mechanisms for mapping software components to hardware components, an interactive simulator for prototype interpretation, and a reuse capability. The simulator contains components for instrumenting, animating, debugging, and displaying results of functional and performance models. The Pproto environment is built on top of a substrate for managing user interfaces and database objects to provide consistent views of design objects across system tools.

Key Words: parallel processing, parallel programming, rapid prototyping, computer-aided software engineering (CASE), software/hardware architectures, visual programming

1. Introduction

Advances in computational power and availability continue to increase the attractiveness of employing parallel architectures in high-performance applications. Unfortunately, architecting of software systems to exploit the performance afforded by these processors remains a difficult challenge for software engineers. Use of parallel machines complicates the specification and implementation problem because of the potentially large design space that needs to be explored in order to meet functional and performance requirements. Lack of tools for analyzing high-level software and hardware architectural trade-offs contributes to the difficulties faced by system analysts.

It is at the architectural design levels where design decisions can have significant impact on the eventual functionality and performance of parallel systems. Thus, methodologies and tools for analyzing prototypes during early phases of the specification and design process are critical to meeting system requirements. In the design of systems centered around parallel processing, design environments must encompass mechanisms for curtailing the inherent complexity introduced by the need to handle multiple concurrent computation threads. Graphical visualization techniques must be extended to provide powerful tools for codesign of software and hardware architectures.

Parallel Proto (PProto) is a computer-aided software engineering (CASE) environment that aims to overcome difficulties associated with building parallel programs by supporting construction of such programs with rapid prototyping techniques. The objective of the

PProto project is to investigate and develop a methodology and associated tools for the formal definition, analysis, and validation of specifications, designs, and implementations of system architectures incorporating both parallel and sequential processing elements [1,2].

The PProto prototyping environment concentrates on integration of techniques for codesign and analysis of high-level software and hardware architectures. The system supports mechanisms for specifying scheduling, concurrency, data dependencies, synchronization, and performance characteristics of multiple processing threads. Using prototyping as the primary methodology for engineering parallel and distributed software systems, PProto addresses the following areas:

1. *Specification and design of software prototypes.* Rapid system design is achieved with a visual hierarchical dataflow language with facilities for dynamic object-oriented data modeling. A sophisticated dataflow graph editor provides the support for creating and editing system prototypes.
2. *Architecture modeling.* A graphical architecture editor is provided for building resource models of many types of multiple-instruction, multiple-data stream (MIMD) machines, including shared-memory and distributed-memory systems. Facilities are available for mapping of software (logical) components to hardware (physical) components.
3. *Prototype execution using simulation.* Subsystems to support execution of prototypes include an interpreter, a scheduler, and an architecture modeler. Additional simulation support includes tools for interactive debugging, functional animation, and instrumentation for functional and performance analysis.
4. *Design reuse.* Management and browsing of libraries containing reusable specifications and designs is integrated with the system editors.
5. *User interface management.* Interfaces to editing and simulation tools are managed by a common graphical interface substrate. The user interface manager guarantees a clear and consistent interface across tools.
6. *Object management.* Management of persistent objects is implemented by an object-oriented database commonly accessible to all system tools.

PProto is being developed through a set of modifications and enhancements to Proto+, a prototyping tool for specification and design of software systems based on dataflow concepts [3]. Proto+, in turn, extends the functional prototyping capabilities of the RADC Proto System [4] with a model for concurrent processing and communication that provides control over scheduling of operations.

Subsequent sections of this paper are structured as follows. Section 2 discusses related work in environments for parallel programming. Section 3 describes capabilities of PProto that distinguishes it from previous efforts and presents a tool and methodological overview of the system. Details of the primary functional systems of PProto are described in Section 4. Section 5 contains an electronic funds transfer example to motivate usage scenarios of the environment. Finally, Section 6 concludes with a description of the current system status and outlines future directions of PProto involving the use of visualization techniques for performance analysis.

2. Related Work: Parallel Programming Environments

Current and future advances in multiprocessor technology are expected to increase the need for integrated software engineering environments for parallel and distributed programming. In order to exploit computational power of multiprocessor systems, the PProto environment assists analysts in explicit specification of parallelism, debugging of multiple processing threads, and evaluation of performance and efficiency. This section reviews other work in the area of parallel programming environments.

Application of advanced visual interfaces to detailed implementation and performance evaluation of parallel systems has been the focus of several research efforts. ParaScope assists in the formulation, implementation, automatic parallelization, computation scheduling, and debugging of parallel Fortran programs [5]. The Parallel Programming and Instrumentation Environment (PIE) focuses on visualization of concurrent program performance for debugging and supports analysis, verification, and validation of a computation's performance [6]. In Faust, the emphasis is on an integrated environment for scientific applications that includes database, data and control analysis, restructuring, program maintenance, and performance analysis components [7]. IPS-2 is a program measurement system that supports instrumentation and analysis techniques that guide a programmer to the source of program bottlenecks [8].

The graphical visualization capabilities available in these environments is impressive, allowing them to be employed effectively for tuning of parallel algorithms. Using invasive procedures, statistics are gathered dynamically while a system is running. These statistics are subsequently manipulated via interactive visual displays to present measurements such as context switching, parallelism, and procedure calls. The emphasis on system details, however, makes these environments inadequate for analyzing high-level architectural trade-offs. That is, once a design has reached a level of detail that is appropriate for implementation and analysis with these tools, it has already been fully architected and it is too late to make architectural modifications without having to reimplement significant portions of the design.

Support for higher-level visual program abstractions and code reuse is available in CODE [9,10]. This system is capable of automatically generating code for several target parallel machines and languages. CODE, however, concentrates on the logical aspects of program design and reuse; little consideration is given to logical-to-physical mapping and performance modeling aspects of software architectures.

AXE is a software testbed for evaluating multiprocessor architectures, related resource management strategies, concurrent problem formulation, and dynamic load balancing algorithms [11,12]. The system supports investigations in these areas using discrete time simulation and graphical visualization tools. Although AXE's integrated environment and methodology is similar to PProto in some respects, it emphasizes presentation of simulation results and lacks a visual software specification interface.

The PAWS (Parallel Assessment Window System) evaluation tool for parallel systems provides an interactive environment for analysis of existing, prototype, and conceptual architectures running a common application [13]. The system includes tools for characterization of applications, architecture selection, performance assessment, and graphical display of results. These tools differ from those of PProto in several important aspects: (1) application input to PAWS is a high-level language (currently Ada), in PProto, applications are explicitly developed within the environment using hierarchical dataflow graphs, (2) performance characterization in PAWS is accomplished with analytic techniques, PProto uses simulation, and (3) software and hardware models in PAWS are at relatively detailed levels of abstraction, PProto uses coarse-grained models.

General purpose simulation tools [14,15] can also be employed for parallel programming. Use of such tools, however, requires the analyst to explicitly program in a simulation language many of the generic software/hardware modeling and performance analysis aspects of system design, a difficult and time-consuming activity. Development of this component infrastructure takes place in addition to domain modeling tasks associated with application specifications. One can even go a step below simulation tools and directly employ general purpose programming languages, such as C or Ada, for software/hardware modeling. Resorting to these low-level programming abstractions multiplies the difficulties and disadvantages of using general purpose simulation tools.

3. Prototyping Parallel Programs with PProto

PProto is a tool used by system analysts to accomplish the following:

- Create functional specifications.
- Refine functional specifications into interpretable functional prototypes.
- Interactively debug functional prototypes.
- Execute the functional prototypes before knowledgeable end users to validate the proposed functionality in the context of target systems.
- Construct models of parallel machine architectures.
- Evaluate the performance of different mappings of functional prototypes onto parallel machines.

3.1. Functional Overview

The PProto visualization/editing and simulation tools are closely tied to a database object manager, allowing tools to share objects and screen images with consistent interpretations. This relationship is depicted in the high-level dataflow diagram of Figure 1. In addition to communicating via persistent objects, the visualization/editing and simulation tools are directly linked by exchanging control information and simulation results. The simulation tools employ graphical displays of the visualization/editing tools to present functional and performance execution results.

A PProto system specification is a hierarchical dataflow graph consisting of process *nodes*, *data stores*, communication *connections*, and *ports* (which constitute the interface between nodes and connections). Each node in the hierarchy may be structurally specified by a refinement, which is itself a dataflow graph. This nested graph receives all its inputs and sends all its outputs to the ports on its enclosing node. The *behavior* of each leaf node of a graph, where a leaf node is a node that contains no further refinement, is described with a simple structured programming language whose statements are interpreted by PProto.

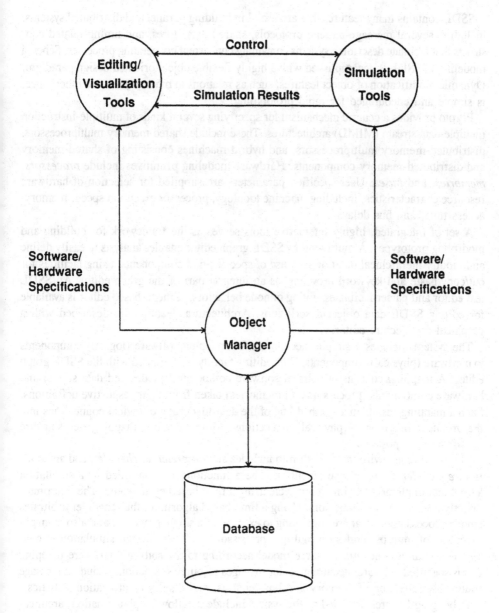

Figure 1. High-level dataflow in PProto.

PProto's software modeling language is called the System Specification and Design Language (SSDL). In the SSDL language, a clear distinction is made between the following portions of a design:

- *Dataflow.* Graphical model of a specification.
- *Behavior.* Data transformations effected by leaf nodes of a dataflow graph.
- *Schema.* Dynamic object-oriented data definitions.

SSDL contains many features that are useful in building parallel and distributed systems, including several message-passing protocols, shared data stores, and timing-related constructs that facilitate describing systems containing concurrent cooperating processes. Schema modeling in SSDL is accomplished with a highly flexible object-oriented design paradigm. Dynamic modification of object features, such as relations to other objects and inheritance, is simple and encouraged for rapid prototyping.

PProto provides a generic mechanism for specifying several kinds of multiple-instruction multiple-data stream (MIMD) architectures. These include shared-memory multiprocessors, distributed-memory multiprocessors, and hybrid machines consisting of shared-memory and distributed-memory components. Hardware modeling primitives include *processors*, *memories*, and *buses*. User-specified parameters are supplied for selection of hardware resource characteristics, including machine topology, processor execution speed, memory-access time, and bus delay.

A set of integrated, highly interactive tools serves as the framework for building and modifying prototypes. A multiwindow SSDL graph editor enables analysts to easily define and modify hierarchical dataflows. Reuse of specification components, using facilities for cut/copy/paste and keyword browsing, is an integral part of the graph editor. An SSDL text editor and parser facilitates editing of node behaviors. A menu-based editor is available for editing SSDL data object descriptions. Architectural features are described with a graphical architecture editor.

The system includes a simple mechanism for mapping software (logical) components to hardware (physical) components. This editing facility is integrated with the SSDL graph editor. A mapping consists of pairs of software components (nodes and data stores) and hardware components (processors and memories) taken from their respective definitions. Such a mapping results in an embedding of the dataflow graph of logical connections into the architecture graph of physical connections. More than one mapping per software specification is possible.

The simulation environment in PProto includes an *interpreter*, a *scheduler*, and an *architecture modeler* for prototype execution. These functions are controlled by a simulation kernel that implements a simulation cycle using a time-based event queue. The interpreter directly executes SSDL behaviors. Using a time-based algorithm, the scheduler arbitrates among process nodes that are competing to execute on a single processor and also manages execution of multiple nodes on multiple processors. Software design simulation is constrained by an architecture resource model according to the software/hardware mapping that is specified. The architecture modeler manages resource simulation, including message routing, serialization of memory and bus requests, and display of utilization statistics.

Debugging features provided by the system include dataflow graph animation, architecture animation, breakpoints, single stepping of behaviors, data display instruments, resource utilization instruments, data browsing, and automatic deadlock detection for parallel specifications.

3.2. Methodology Overview

Key to successful use of PProto is the integrated support for methods and procedures that lead to good software engineering of parallel systems. Important factors that influence the prototyping methodology of PProto include:

1. *Prototyping capabilities*. SSDL addresses functional, structural, timing, and behavioral issues. Consequently, it is possible to develop multiple versions of a system prototype in order to address different types of questions.
2. *Concurrent execution model*. The PProto concurrent execution model supports prototyping of systems consisting of multiple communicating processes running on multiprocessors.
3. *Emphasis on reuse*. PProto reuse strategy encourages top-down incremental development through early identification of reusable components.
4. *Resource model*. Architectural resource impacts can be identified in order to determine prototype performance characteristics. The system facilitates performing software/hardware mapping tradeoffs.
5. *Simulation capabilities*. A sophisticated set of simulation utilities for interpretation, scheduling, resource modeling, instrumentation, animation, and debugging of prototypes supports careful analysis of system functions and performance.

Figure 2 illustrates how these factors are incorporated into the PProto methodology flow diagram. A system analyst begins by translating requirements into a high-level dataflow specification. Dataflows, behaviors, and data models of the specification are refined using various SSDL editing tools to yield a detailed functional prototype. This prototype is simulated using the interpreter to verify that its function properly meets requirements.

Following functional prototyping, resource modeling of alternative hardware architectures to be used as delivery platforms takes place. Typically, these models will have been developed previously, so the analyst just needs to select candidate architectures suitable for the specification being designed. Subsequently, one or more mappings from the functional prototype to each candidate architecture prototype is defined. These mappings are used for simulation of performance prototypes. Simulation results yield important metrics for performing cost/performance trade-offs.

The methodology is strongly dependent on the reuse of design artifacts, including specifications, architectures, data models, and behaviors. The system's underlying substrate for managing user interfaces and database objects guarantees consistent views of design artifacts across system tools. Consequently, integrated support for the methodology, tools, and reuse capability is built into the system.

The methodology is based on repeated iteration back to any step of the specification and design process. This supports an incremental design approach whereby activities such as adapting to changing requirements and modifying specifications for different decompositions of requirements are accommodated in the design process. Since functional prototypes are executable, convenient points are available throughout the process steps to incorporate user validation of the prototype being constructed.

4. PProto Design

The integrated tools of PProto allow rapid system prototyping for functional specification validation. This capability reduces errors in defining requirements for proposed systems, which subsequently reduces the cost and risk involved in developing such systems. Additionally, PProto contains functionality for architectural resource modeling and software/hardware

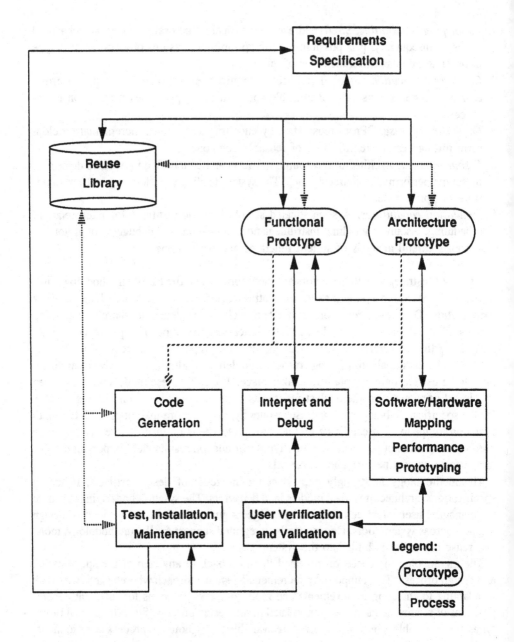

Figure 2. PProto methodology flow diagram.

mapping to support analysis of system prototype performance characteristics. This section describes the design of PProto in terms of architecture and dataflow, software and hardware specification languages, and system tools.

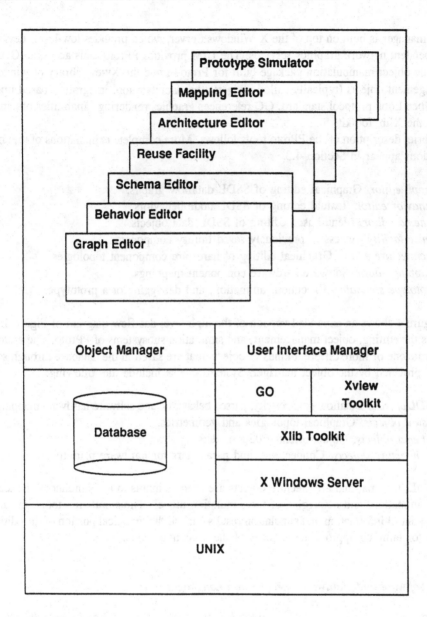

Figure 3. PProto architecture.

4.1. Architecture and Dataflow

Figure 3 depicts PProto's architecture. The system is implemented in C++ on top of the UNIX^TM operating system. Database management services are provided by the *object manager*, which is built on top of a commercial object-oriented database. The *user interface manager* (UIM) supplies graphical and textual interface services to most system tools.

This manager is built on top of the X Windows Server, which provides low-level, device-independent network graphics services. The UIM provides PProto tools access to GO, a graphic object manipulation package built for Proto+, and the Xview library of window management objects (typically called widgets) that facilitate tool integration based upon the Open Look protocol standard. GO references graphics rendering capabilities obtained from the Xlib Toolkit.

A brief description of the PProto tools follows. More complete explanations of the tool functions appear in Section 4.3.

1. *Graph editor.* Graphical editing of SSDL dataflow graphs.
2. *Behavior editor.* Textual editing of SSDL node behaviors.
3. *Schema editor.* Menu-based editing of SSDL data objects.
4. *Reuse facility.* Access to previously saved library components.
5. *Architecture editor.* Graphical editing of hardware component topologies.
6. *Mapping editor.* Software/hardware component mappings.
7. *Prototype simulator.* Execution, animation, and debugging of a prototype.

Figure 4 shows an expanded version of the high-level dataflow diagram of Figure 1. It shows the editing, object management, and simulation subsystems of PProto. The editors generate one or more different kinds of objects that are saved in the database through services provided by the object manager. System objects include the following:

1. *SSDL objects.* Dataflow connectivity, parsed behaviors, and software/hardware mappings.
2. *Visual objects.* Graphical topologies and geometries.
3. *Schema objects.* Object-oriented data models.
4. *Architecture objects.* Connectivity and parameters for hardware primitives.

SSDL, schema, and architecture objects are used as inputs to the simulator for execution, animation, and debugging of the simulation model. The simulation tools, in turn, relay control information and simulation results back to the graphical portion of the editing tools for building appropriate displays of the execution status.

4.2. Software and Hardware Specification Languages

In PProto, a clear distinction is made between specifications of software and hardware. This section describes the software and hardware modeling primitives available in the system.

4.2.1. Software Specification Using SSDL. An SSDL software system specification is a hierarchical dataflow graph that contains of the following primitives:

• *Nodes.* Concurrent processes, functions, operators.
• *Data stores.* Shared memory to store state information.
• *Connections.* Communication channels between nodes and data stores.
• *Ports.* Interfaces between nodes and connections.

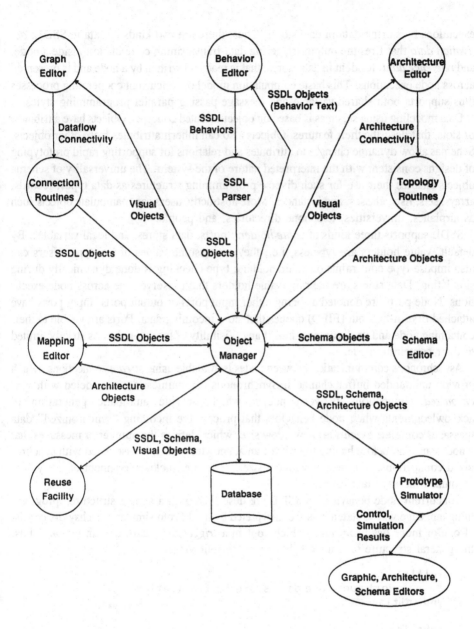

Figure 4. PProto dataflow diagram.

Each node in the hierarchy may be structurally specified by a decomposition, or refinement, which is itself a dataflow graph. This nested graph receives all its inputs and sends all its outputs to the ports on its enclosing node. The *behavior* of each leaf node of a graph defines the functional transformation that takes place inside a node.

A dataflow description corresponds to a functional specification, where dataflow nodes denote stateless system functions. Data are transient and passes from node to node along connections in the form of messages. It is possible, however, to preserve state across node executions by storing data in data stores. Thus, there are two kinds of data in SSDL: *activation data* that fires the output-triggering data-transforming computation inside a node, and *reference data*, resident in data stores, that is read and written by a node and is preserved across node executions. This basic computation model of concurrent cooperating processes thus supports both shared-variable and message-passing parallel programming styles.

Data modeling using schemas is based on object-oriented concepts. Objects have attributes, or slots, that describe their features. Objects also can inherit attributes from other objects. Schemas allow dynamic changes to attributes and relations for supporting rapid prototyping of designs consistent with the interpreted nature of the system. The universality of schema objects enables their use for such diverse programming structures as data types, records, arrays, sets, lists, classes, and instances. More abstractly, users can manipulate objects such as airplanes, universities, telephone directories, and people.

SSDL supports three kinds of *value holders*: ports, data stores, and local variables. By default, value holders are typeless, i.e., they can assume values of any type. Users can also impose type constraints on value holders; type checking is done dynamically during simulation. Data stores are the only value holders that preserve state across node executions. Node ports are denoted as being either input ports or output ports. Input ports have attached first-in-first-out (FIFO) queues that store incoming data. Ports are visible to their containing node and its decomposition, if any. Visibility of local variables is strictly limited to their containing node.

Asynchronous communication between nodes is available using *stream* connections, which provide unbounded buffer channels. Synchronous communication is modeled with *synchronized* connections between nodes, which provide automatic generation of acknowledgments when node behaviors that process the incoming "synchronized" data messages complete execution. A window size, which defines the number of messages that a node can send before having to wait for an acknowledgment, is associated with synchronized connections. The default window size is one; i.e., acknowledgment of every synchronized message takes place.

Concurrent node behaviors in SSDL are described with a simple structured programming language whose statements are interpreted by the PProto simulator. Behaviors consist of one or more *behavior rules*, which contain a *trigger*, or guard, and an *action*. Thus, the general structure of a node behavior is the following:

```
initial
        -- Port queue and data store initialization.
end initial

behavior
        <trigger1> :- <action1> !
        <trigger2> :- <action2> !
        ...
        <triggerN> :- <actionN> !
end behavior
```

If a trigger expression is empty, the behavior rule is said to be an *independent* behavior, otherwise, the behavior rule is a *dependent* behavior. Conditional triggers for dependent behaviors may have one of the following forms:

```
accept <input port name>
<trigger expression> or <trigger expression>
<trigger expression> and <trigger expression>
```

Thus, triggers specify how data messages are accepted, or received, by a node (i.e., **accept** operations) and the input data conditions under which a node is activated, or fires. Even though the triggers of multiple behavior rules within a node may be true simultaneously, at most one behavior rule within a node can be executing at any given time. In this manner, use of the behavior rule construct allows specification of nondeterministic selection of alternative actions, which subsequently influences scheduling decisions during simulation.

High-level SSDL constructs for specifying behavior rule actions include iteration, conditional statements, assignment, message-passing primitives, value holder accesses, timing constraints, and schema object interfaces. Behavior constructs are also available to initialize port queues and data stores, and provide access to procedures written in external languages, such as C. Built-in functions are available for displaying data values, delaying behavior execution an arbitrary number of simulation time units, and accessing the global simulation clock, as well as other procedures useful for simulation debugging.

A **read** operation for a value holder is carried out whenever the value holder is referenced in evaluating an expression (e.g., the expression on the right-hand side of an assignment statement or a conditional expression in an iteration statement). Value holder **write** operations occur whenever the value holder appears on the left-hand side of an assignment statement. Read and write access from nodes to data stores is achieved over *access* connections.

Within behavior rule actions, sending of data through output ports is accomplished with **supply** operations, whose syntax is as follows:

```
supply <output port name> ;
```

Alternatively, the **store-send** operator is used as a shorthand to assign a value to an output port and supply the port. Its syntax is

```
<output port name> << <expression> ;
```

which is equivalent to

```
<output port name> := <expression> ;
supply <output port name> ;
```

Data stores are marked with a *lock* attribute that can be used to restrict concurrent access (data store **read** and **write** operations) to the data store in such a manner as to prevent data corruption. In particular, when the lock attribute is set for a given data store, the system enforces the following rules

* *Exclusive writer.* At most one behavior rule can write a data store simultaneously.
* *Multiple readers.* Zero or more behavior rules can read a data store simultaneously as long as there is no other behavior rule writing to it.

• *Data store acquisition*. A behavior rule acquires **read** or **write** access privileges to all the data stores it needs prior to execution; it releases the data store privileges after completing execution.

This protocol treats behavior rules as critical regions for the purpose of concurrent access to data stores, which automatically enforces more discipline in the construction of parallel and distributed programming applications.

4.2.2. Hardware Specification. PProto provides a generic mechanism for specifying parallel and distributed MIMD architectures. These include shared-memory multiprocessors, distributed-memory multiprocessors, and hybrid machines consisting of shared-memory and distributed-memory components. Hardware resource modeling primitives include:

• *Processors*. Execute node behaviors.
• *Memories*. Contain data store values.
• *Buses*. Transfer messages for node communication and data store accesses.

Users are free to specify any machine topology consisting of these components. The only topological restrictions are that buses must be used to connect processors to other processors or to memories; i.e., processors and memories cannot be directly connected to each other.

User-specified parameters for selection of hardware resource characteristics include processor execution speed, read and write memory-access times, and message delays. All these parameters are defined in terms of simulation time units. Specification of processor execution speed involves designating delays for the following behavior operations:

add/subtract	—addition and subtraction
accept	—stream and synchronized
assign	—writing of value holders
c_call	—calls to external C functions
divide	—division
jump	—if, loop, and exit statements
index	—array indexing
logical_op	—not, or, and
multiply	—multiplication
new	—creation of new and copied schemas
read	—reading of value holders
relational_op	—>, >=, <, <=, =, !=
attribute	—access to schema attributes
stop	—stop statement
supply	—stream and synchronized

Static minimum delay routing between primitives is automatically computed by the system using Floyd's shortest path algorithm [16]. During simulation, these routings are used to process message-passing (**supply**) and data-store access (**read/write**) requests as high-level constructs. Consequently, a software design and does not have to be changed when it is ported from one architecture to another, or when different software/hardware mappings are used for the same architecture. For example, a software specification that assumes a logical shared-memory model can be mapped onto a shared-memory multiprocessor or a distributed-memory multiprocessor without changing any code. In the latter case, the physical model is one of distributed shared memory.

4.3. Tool Descriptions

Based on Figures 3 and 4, the following sections cover principal functional components of PProto in detail.

4.3.1. Graph Editor.
Dataflow graphs in SSDL are created and modified with a multiwindow graph editor. This is an object-oriented editor in that a user first selects an object (i.e., node, data store, connection, port) and then selects the action to be performed on that object. Graphical object operations include inserting, moving, deleting, labeling, and connecting objects. The editor supports composition of nodes into hierarchical dataflow refinements. Other graphical facilities available in the editor include fast-path options (i.e., performing several equivalent operations simultaneously), descriptive built-in icons, user-specified instruments, panning, zooming, and scrolling.

Visual objects, which contain topological and geometrical information related to dataflow graphs, are generated directly by the graph editor for storage in the database. These objects are built incrementally and are subject to certain graphical syntax checks. Graph connectivity information, which also is generated incrementally, is supplied to connectivity routines that build SSDL objects.

The graph editor provides integrated access to other subsystems, including the behavior editor, the schema editor, the reuse facility, and the mapping editor. Graphical cut-and-paste and copy-and-paste operations are provided for reuse purposes. In addition, the graph editor windows are used during simulation for animation, instrumentation, and debugging.

4.3.2. Behavior Editor.
Behaviors for SSDL nodes are constructed using a text editor that is accessible from the graph editor. This editor implements syntax templates in the form menus for SSDL language constructs and available library functions that assist users in developing programs. A parser for SSDL behaviors, which generates SSDL objects, is integrated with the behavior editor. SSDL text also is saved as part of the SSDL object structures. Input and output access to files also is available in the behavior editor.

4.3.2. Schema Editor.
A menu-based editor provides structured access to creation and modification of schema objects. Schema features that can be modified include attributes, inheritance, and attribute initialization. Integrated access to this editor can be obtained from the graph editor to create and modify schema information for SSDL language constructs that involve data, such as data stores and local variables.

4.3.4. Architecture Editor.
PProto users edit architecture definitions using an object-oriented, window-based graphical architecture editor. Like the dataflow graph editor, editing operations in the architecture editor consist of selecting an object (i.e., processor, memory, bus)

followed by selecting the action to be performed on that object. These actions include inserting, moving, resizing, rotating, deleting, labeling, and connecting objects. Other graphical facilities available in the editor include fast-path options, panning, zooming, and scrolling.

Topological and geometrical information related to hardware configurations is generated directly by the architecture editor for storage in the database as visual objects. These objects are built incrementally and are subject to certain graphical syntax checks. In addition, incrementally generated architecture connectivity information is supplied to routines that build architecture objects.

4.3.5. Mapping Editor. Architectural resource models are incorporated into software models by establishing mappings from software (logical) components to hardware (physical) components. The mapping editor is integrated into the graph editor and is built from interactive menus. Mappings describe a software/hardware allocation and consist of (node, processor) and (data store, memory) pairs. Thus, mappings are embeddings of dataflow graphs into resource graphs. More than one mapping can be specified for a given dataflow graph. The mapping editor automatically performs consistency and completeness checks to detect illegal mappings. For example, attempts to map a node to a memory or a data store to a processor are flagged as illegal. In addition, the mapping editor supports heuristic and random algorithms for automatic allocation of software components to hardware components.

Typically, mappings in PProto are defined in the context of an explicitly specified architecture definition. For early stages of functional prototype development, the mapping facility also supports default sequential and fully parallel mappings. In the *sequential mapping*, all nodes are mapped to a single processor (i.e., node executions are serialized), all data stores are mapped to a single memory that has read and write access times of zero simulation time units, and the processor is connected to the memory by a zero-delay bus. In the *fully parallel mapping*, each node is mapped to its own processor, all data stores are mapped to a single memory that has read-and-write access times of zero simulation time units, and the processors are connected to the memory by a zero-delay bus. The fully parallel mapping models true dataflow execution.

4.3.6. Reuse Facility. Invocation of the reuse facility is achieved through the graph editor. Reusable library components can be located through keyword searching with user-specified accuracy. Copy-and-paste and cut-and-paste operations are the primary means for inserting components from one design into another. In addition to component location and insertion, the reuse facility also contains functionality for saving components in reuse libraries.

For cut-and-copy operations, a design component is defined as a process node plus its behaviors, ports, and refinements (including internal nodes, behaviors, ports, data stores, and channels). Cut-and-copy operations can be performed within a single database and from one database to another. The latter permits easy access to sharing of reusable components between users.

4.3.7. Prototype Simulator. The key to prototype analysis and performance evaluation is the simulation environment available in PProto. Prototype execution is implemented by a simulator consisting of a simulation kernel, interpreter, scheduler, and architecture modeler.

The simulator uses the graphical interfaces of the graphic, architecture, and schema editors to display simulation results, although prototype editing is disabled during execution.

Simulation Cycle. The simulation kernel implements the simulation cycle, which is the backbone that references other components of the simulator. An efficient calendar event queue structure manages all time-ordered events generated by the system [17].

The interpreter executes all behavior constructs and keeps track of execution time according to processor operation delays. The interpreter also generates events for message-passing and data-store accesses. Another function of the interpreter is to collect execution statistics, such as counting the number of times a node is executed.

The simulator includes an architecture modeler that performs the tasks of memory and bus serialization, message and memory-access routing, and hardware statistics collection. Although memory and bus requests are serialized by the architecture modeler, the scheduler is responsible for serializing node requests for processor resources. The scheduler makes use of node activation times, execution counts, and node priorities to arbitrate among multiple nodes competing to execute on a single processor. It also manages scheduling multiple parallel processors, although this does not involve sophisticated functionality because software/hardware allocation is specified statically.

The flow diagram in Figure 5 illustrates the cycle employed by PProto's simulation kernel. *Tnow* denotes the current simulation time. The simulation ends when either there are no more events to process or the user-specified time limit has been exceeded. Otherwise, the update and execution phases are executed.

In the *update phase*, `supply`, `read` data store, and `write` data store events are forwarded to the architecture modeler, which is responsible for enqueueing `supply` values on destination ports. Also, processors for all completed behaviors are freed. Subsequently, the scheduler is called to assign behaviors to free processors. This requires checking behavior rule triggers, which are dependent on port queue contents. Functionality to animate the graphical display and process breakpoints is also contained in the update phase.

In scheduling behavior rules competing to execute on a single processor, the scheduling algorithm gives dependent behavior rules precedence over independent behavior rules. Among dependent behavior rules, those belonging to nodes with higher priority and having earlier activation time and lower execution count, in that order, have higher precedence. The activation time of a behavior rule is the time at which the rule's trigger first becomes true; the execution count measures the number of times a behavior rule has executed. Precedence among independent behavior rules is similarly determined according to node priorities and execution counts.

The *execution phase* calls the interpreter for each scheduled behavior. The interpreter may be called more than once in the execution phase since there may be multiple processors, each executing a different behavior. In effect, this is how simulation of parallel processors is achieved. Interpretation of a behavior usually results in generation of more `supply`, `read`, and `write` events, which trigger subsequent executions of the simulation cycle.

Debugging Support. Graphical instrumentation of a prototype simulation is an important function of the simulator. Dynamic mechanisms for assisting users in observing prototype

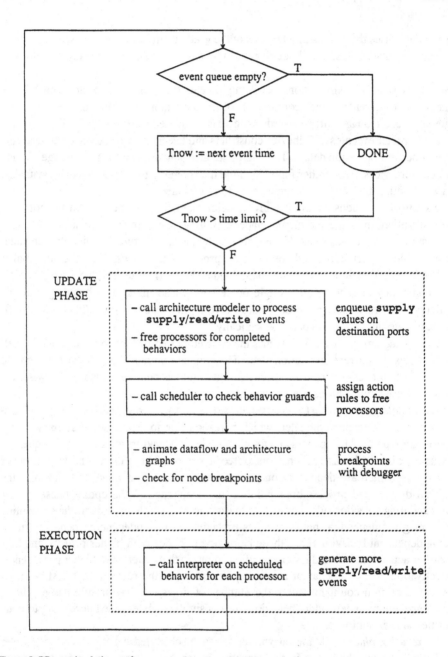

Figure 5. PProto simulation cycle.

execution include dataflow graph animation (e.g., highlighting of nodes and connections), textual data displays, special-purpose graphical displays (e.g., queue-status icons), general-purpose displays (e.g., thermometers for displaying resource utilization statistics, text windows to display message data), and data traces. Display features of these mechanisms are tailorable by users.

In addition to instrumentation, several other debugging mechanisms are available. For example, the system supports setting breakpoints before and after node execution, single-stepping, execution of the SSDL display statement (for printing port, data store, variable, node, object values), and interrupting the simulation. Furthermore, most objects in the system, such as nodes, connections, ports, data stores, processors, memories, and buses, can be examined when prototype simulation is suspended. A tool for automatic detection of deadlocks in parallel specifications is also available. This facility employs an incremental algorithm to detect deadlocks among nodes communicating via synchronized connections and sharing locked data stores.

Combined with a listing of comprehensive node, processor, memory, and bus statistics generated at the end of simulation, the incremental debugging and evaluation facilities provide effective support for high-level architectural trade-off analysis.

4.3.8. User Interface Manager (UIM). The UIM collects user inputs and distributes them to appropriate tools. The UIM also manages the multiwindow display screen. In this manner, PProto keeps a clean separation between user-interface functions and application functions that operate on application data. Consequently, the system shields tool applications from modifications and enhancements to the user interface.

During a PProto session, all inputs either come from the PProto database or interactive user input from either a keyboard or a mouse. User interaction follows the object-then-action paradigm. With this paradigm, the user is presented with a display containing a collection of objects. A mouse is used to select the desired object, and the system responds by presenting a menu of actions that are acceptable for the selected object. The user then selects the desired action from the menu. This reduces burden on the analyst of remembering command syntax and performing unnecessary keyboard entry. Mandatory keyboard use is primarily restricted to entering alphanumeric data strings required by PProto tools (e.g., graphic object names, comments, reuse keywords), behavior portion of SSDL, and attributes and values of schema objects.

PProto outputs usually are written to the PProto database or presented to the user on a display screen. Outputs to the screen are in the form of graphical displays inside windows, menus, and alphanumeric displays. Descriptive graphical depiction of data is preferred; textual displays are limited to situations where text has served as user input and where text is the most natural notation for presenting output (e.g., error messages). File input and output is available from several PProto tools.

4.3.9. Object Manager. PProto uses an object-oriented database, or object base, to manage persistence and sharing of system artifacts, including SSDL, architecture, and visual objects. The object manager provides an application-level interface for controlled access to the database, as well as facilities for configuration management and version control. PProto supports simultaneous access to multiple databases by multiple users in order to acquire reusable component libraries.

5. Usage Scenario: Electronic Funds Transfer Example

Several of the parallel programming elements of the PProto methodology are now illustrated using a simple example involving the architecture and design of a distributed electronic funds transfer (EFT) system. This example is based on a design presented in [18]. The EFT system processes *transactions* involving the automatic transfer of funds from *customer accounts* to *merchant accounts*.

5.1. SSDL Implementation of the EFT Specification

The following three kinds of nodes are used in the EFT system:

1. *Terminal*. Originates new transactions and notifies customer whether transactions are accepted or rejected.
2. *Bank*. Debits customer accounts and credits merchant accounts according to transaction requests.
3. *Switch*. Routes transactions between terminals and banks according to customer and merchant account numbers and transaction status.

A transaction originates at a point-of-sale terminal and contains information regarding the transfer amount, customer account number, and merchant account number. When a transaction arrives at the switch from a terminal, it is routed to the appropriate customer bank. Subsequently, the bank then either accepts the transaction and debits the customer account with the amount of the transaction, or rejects the transaction if there are insufficient funds in the customer account. The bank then forwards the transaction to the switch.

If the transaction was rejected, the switch sends the transaction back to the originating terminal. If the customer bank accepted the transaction, it is routed to the merchant account bank. On arrival at this bank, the merchant account is credited with the transaction amount. The transaction is then sent to the switch for routing back to the originating terminal.

Figure 6 shows the EFT system specification using the visual dataflow portion of SSDL. In addition to the three kinds of nodes mentioned above, there are two types of data stores:

- *AcctToBank*. Array that maps customer and merchant account numbers to banks.
- *Accounts*. List of account numbers and balances contained at a bank.

Definition and initialization of the data types for data stores is done using schema elements in SSDL.

The contents of transactions are also defined using schema. A transaction is a 5-tuple that is an instance of a class containing the following attributes:

1. *Amount*. Requested transfer amount.
2. *Customer__Acct*. Account number of customer.
3. *Merchant__Acct*. Account number of merchant.
4. *Terminal__Id*. Identification of originating terminal
5. *Status*. Either NEW (for new transactions), ACCEPTED (debit took place at customer bank), REJECTED, or DONE (credit took place at merchant bank).

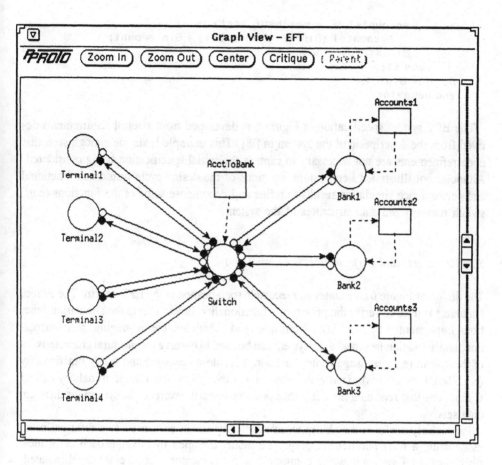

Figure 6. PProto graph editor: EFT example dataflow.

Each node in Figure 6 contains a behavior that is written using the textual portion of SSDL. For example, the behavior assigned to Bank1, whose input and output ports are labeled Bin and Bout, is as follows:

```
behavior
  accept Bin :-
    if (Bin.status = NEW) then
      if (Accounts1(Bin.customer_acct) >= Bin.amount) then
        -- Debit customer account
        Accounts1 (Bin.customer_acct) :=
          Accounts1 (Bin.customer_acct) - Bin.amount;
        Bin.status := ACCEPTED
      else
        -- Reject transaction
        Bin.status := REJECTED
      end if
    else
      -- Credit merchant account
```

```
        Accounts1 (Bin.merchant_acct) :=
            Accounts1 (Bin.merchant_acct) + Bin.amount;
        Bin.status := DONE
    end if;
  Bout << Bin!
  end behavior
```

The EFT system specification in Figure 6 is developed from a set of requirements derived from the description of the system in [18]. This example is simple enough such that node refinements are not necessary to capture the initial specification being considered. Although not illustrated here, future iterations of the design cycle would use functional and performance simulation results to refine and decompose some of the functions (e.g., switch routing) and data structures of the system.

5.2. Functional and Performance Simulation

The design of Figure 6 constitutes an executable specification of the EFT system. The PProto simulator is used to verify the prototype's functionality. In addition to the simulation functions implemented by the SSDL interpreter and scheduler, the debugging, instrumentation, and animation facilities of the system can be used to observe architectural characteristics of the system (e.g., message communication, data store accesses) and verify functionality (e.g., SSDL behaviors). Transaction data enters the system from the terminals by calling C functions that read data files. It is thus possible to easily exercise the system for different data sets.

Particularly useful is the ability to automatically assign each node to a different processor using a fully parallel mapping. The model obtained by this approach is an ideal distributed EFT system in which communication and memory access costs are eliminated. Not only does this allow verifying the functional capabilities of the system, but simulation results can be used to suggest target architectures and software/hardware mappings that are best matched to the EFT architecture. Also, such prototyping helps identify serial bottlenecks that can be reduced through further functional changes.

Performance simulation typically involves mapping a software specification to one or more hardware architecture definitions. Several mappings and architectures are suggested in Figures 7–9. Note that although these architectures have in some cases radically different underlying models, it is unnecessary to change the specification in order to map it to any of them. As discussed previously, routing of message passing and memory access operations are automatically handled by the system.

Table 1 contains simulation time measurements for these architectures using the same transaction input data. Measurements for the default sequential and fully parallel architectures are also included. The same processor model is employed for each architecture. Results of three simulation runs are shown for the shared-memory, distributed-memory, and hybrid machines using bus and memory access delays of 0, 1, and 10 simulation time units.

By observing resource utilization and performance characteristics of the combined software/hardware models, analysts can identify advantages and disadvantages of different system architectures in early phases of the specification and design cycle. Performance simulation

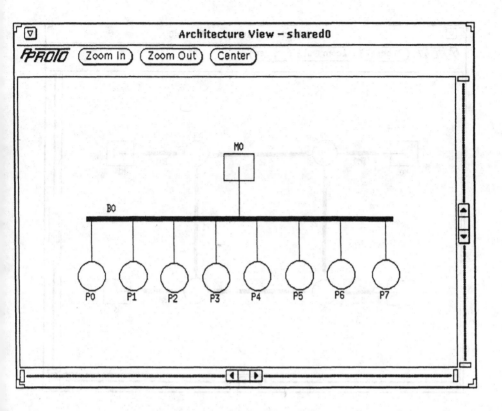

(Terminal1, P0)	(Bank2, P6)
(Terminal2, P1)	(Bank3, P7)
(Terminal3, P2)	(AcctToBank, M0)
(Terminal4, P3)	(Accounts1, M0)
(Switch, P4)	(Accounts2, M0)
(Bank1, P5)	(Accounts3, M0)

Figure 7. EFT mapping to shared memory machine.

may also suggest functional changes that can reduce serial bottlenecks in parallel and distributed systems. For example, with bus-and-memory access times of 0 units, simulation time for the fully parallel architecture is the same as that of the shared-memory and hybrid machines. The distributed-memory machine takes longer due to the allocation of two nodes to each processor. Simulation times for the three machines are approximately the same when bus and memory access times of 1 unit are employed—bus utilization is negligible in all three machines.

Once access times are increased to 10 time units, bus utilization for the shared-memory machine jumps to 90%, which accounts for the additional simulation time used by this machine. On the other hand, even though the distributed-memory machine has only half of the processors available in the hybrid machine, its performance is competitive due to greater bus connectivity and balanced node distribution.

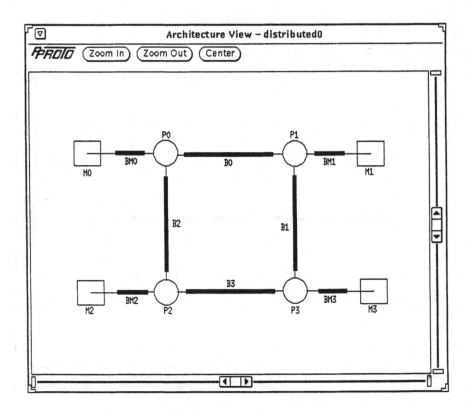

(Terminal1, P0)	(Bank2, P2)
(Terminal2, P1)	(Bank3, P3)
(Terminal3, P2)	(AcctToBank, M0)
(Terminal4, P3)	(Accounts1, M1)
(Switch, P0)	(Accounts2, M2)
(Bank1, P1)	(Accounts3, M3)

Figure 8. EFT mapping to distributed memory machine.

6. Conclusions

Parallel Proto (PProto) is a computer-aided software engineering (CASE) environment that overcomes difficulties associated with building parallel programs by supporting construction of such programs with rapid prototyping techniques. Using functional and performance modeling of dataflow specifications, PProto assists in analysis of high-level software and hardware architectural tradeoffs. The system supports mechanisms for specifying scheduling, concurrency, data dependencies, synchronization, and performance characteristics of multiple processing threads.

Integrated facilities provided by PProto include a visual language and an editor for describing hierarchical dataflow graphs, a resource-modeling tool for creating parallel

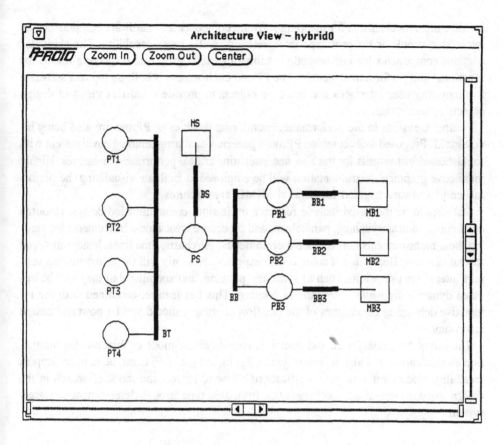

(Terminal1, PT1)	(Bank2, PB2)
(Terminal2, PT2)	(Bank3, PB3)
(Terminal3, PT3)	(AcctToBank, MS)
(Terminal4, PT4)	(Accounts1, MB1)
(Switch, PS)	(Accounts2, MB2)
(Bank1, PB1)	(Accounts3, MB3)

Figure 9. EFT mapping to hybrid machine.

Table 1. EFT example simulation results.

| | Bus/Memory Access Times | | |
Architecture	0 time units	1 time unit	10 time units
Shared-Memory	682	824	2646
Distributed-Memory	742	869	2050
Hybrid	682	812	1964
Default Sequential	1499	—	—
Default Fully-Parallel	682	—	—

architectures, mechanisms for mapping software components to hardware components, an interactive simulator for prototype interpretation, and a reuse capability. The simulator contains components for instrumenting, animating, debugging, and displaying results for functional and performance models. The PProto environment is built on top of a substrate for managing user interfaces and database objects to provide consistent views of design objects across system tools.

Future extensions to the performance monitoring facilities of PProto are also being investigated. Proposed tools combine PProto's generic visual programming environment with sophisticated instruments for tracking and evaluating critical performance measures. Highly interactive graphical instrumentation will be employed to facilitate visualizing the performance of software targeted for parallel MIMD architectures.

Statistics to be measured include resource utilization, communication delays, resource contention, context switching, parallelism, and procedure invocations. Instruments for viewing these measurements may include thermometers, pie charts, time lines, histograms, and textual displays. Heavy use of color is also expected. Not only will these instruments support interactive operations, such as scrolling, panning, and zooming, but they will be updated dynamically *while a program is running*. This last feature, combined with the interactive debugging capabilities of the dataflow language, should yield a powerful design environment.

The use of both interpreted and compiled code in single-mode or mixed-mode simulation and execution will also be investigated. Again, the goal will continue to be to support feasibility studies early in the specifications phase to narrow the scope of search in the design space, as well as a smooth transition from prototype through development of a target system.

Acknowledgments

PProto is being constructed under the sponsorship of the Rome Air Development Center (RADC), Command and Control Division (CO), C^2 Software Technology Branch (COEE), Contract No. F30602-89-C-0129.

References

1. R. D. Acosta, "Simulation of modeling parallel programs in PProto," *Proc. 1991 Summer Comput. Simulation Conf.*, pp. 307–312 July 22–24, 1991.
2. R. D. Acosta and A. Guzmán, "An environment for functional and performance prototyping of parallel programs," *Collected Papers of the 1991 Workshop on Hardware/Software Codesign*, Thirteenth International Conference on Software Engineering, MCC Technical Report No. MCC-CAD-156-91, Microelectronics and Computer Technology Corporation, Austin, TX, May 13, 1991.
3. D. Hartman, "Functional description for the C^3I reusable specification," Air Force Contract No. F30602-88-C-0029, Technical Report No. ISSI-C88A00002-DRAFT, International Software Systems Inc., Austin, TX, June 1989.
4. M. Konrad and D. Hartman, "Functional description for Proto," Air Force Contract No. F30602-85-C-0124, Rome Air Development Center, Griffiss AFB, NY, January 1988.

5. C. D. Callahan, K. D. Cooper, R. T. Hood, K. Kennedy, and L. Torczon, "ParaScope: A parallel programming environment," *Int. J. Supercomput. Appl.* vol. 2, no. 4, pp. 84–99, Winter 1988.

6. T. Lehr, Z. Segall, D. F. Vrsalovic, E. Caplan, A. L. Chung, and C. E. Fineman, "Visualizing performance debugging," *Computer*, vol. 22, no. 10, pp. 38–51, October 1989.

7. V. A. Guarna, D. Gannon, D. Jablonowsky, A. D. Malony, and Y. Gaur, "Faust: An integrated environment for parallel programming," *IEEE Software*, vol. 6, no. 4, pp. 20–26, July 1989.

8. B. P. Miller, M. Clark, J. Hollingsworth, S. Kierstead, S.-S. Lim, and T. Torzewski, "IPS-2: The second generation of a parallel program measurement system," *IEEE Trans. Parallel Dist. Syst.*, vol. 1, no. 2, pp. 206–217, April 1990.

9. J. C. Browne, M. Axam, and S. Sobek, "CODE: A unified approach to parallel programming," *IEEE Software* vol. 6, no. 4, pp. 10–18, July 1989.

10. J. C. Browne, T. Lee, and J. Werth, "Experimental evaluation of a reusability-oriented parallel programming environment," *IEEE Trans. Software Eng.* vol. 16, no. 2, pp. 111–120, February 1990.

11. J. C. Yan, "Post-game analysis–A heuristic resource management framework for concurrent systems," Ph.D. Dissertation, Technical Report No. CSL-TR-88-374, Computer Systems Laboratory, Departments of Electrical Engineering and Computer Science, Stanford University, Stanford, CA, December 1988.

12. J. C. Yan and S. F. Lundstrom, "The post-game analysis framework–Developing resource management strategies for concurrent systems," *IEEE Trans. Knowledge Data Eng.* vol. 1, no. 3, pp. 293–308, September 1989.

13. D. Pease, A. Ghafoor, I. Ahmad, D. L. Andrews, K. Foudil-Bey, T. E. Karpinski, M. Mikki, and M. Zerrouki, "PAWS: A performance evaluation tool for parallel computing systems," *Computer*, vol. 24, no. 1, pp. 18–29, January 1991.

14. SES, "SES/workbench introductory overview," Scientific and Engineering Software, Inc., Austin, TX, April 1989.

15. E. C. Russell, "SIMSCRIPT II.5 and SIMANIMATION: A tutorial," in *Proc. 1987 Winter Simulation Conf.*, A. Thesen, H. Grant, and W. D. Kelton, eds., pp. 102–111, 1987.

16. A. V. Aho, J. E. Hopcroft, and J. D. Ullman, *Data Structures and Algorithms*, Addison-Wesley: Reading, MA, 1983, pp. 208–212.

17. R. Brown, "Calendar queues: A fast O(1) priority queue implementation for the simulation event set problem," *Commun. ACM* vol. 31, no. 10, pp. 1220–1227, October 1988.

18. M. G. Staskauskas, "The formal specification and design of a distributed electronic funds-transfer system," *IEEE Trans. Comput.* vol. 37, no. 12, pp. 1515–1528, December 1988.

Journal of Systems Integration, 1, 367–389 (1991)
© 1991 Kluwer Academic Publishers, Boston. Manufactured in The Netherlands.

Object-Management Machines: Concept and Implementation

BERNHARD HOLTKAMP AND HERBERT WEBER
University of Dortmund, Computer Science/Software Technology, P.O. Box 500 500, D-4600 Dortmund 50, Germany

(Received July 20, 1990; Revised May 14, 1991)

Abstract. The software development process deals with a wide variety of documents. For the preparation of these documents, as well as for their maintenance, appropriate data management support is requested, resulting in the coexistence of multiple object management systems within a single, advanced software development environment. In order to homogenize data management in software development environments we present the object management machine (OMM) concept as an integration framework for preexisting data management systems. An object management machine enables the creation of uniform access patterns to different data management systems, including the query interface and transaction processing. The concept is being developed in the framework of the EUREKA project ESF (EUREKA Software Factory)[1]. To make it operational we demonstrate the suitability of the MUSE multidatabase integrator as an implementation framework for the Object Management Machine concept.

Key Words: Software development environments, distributed systems, object management systems, systems integration.

1. Introduction

The computer supported industrial development of software is meant to be accomplished with software development environments of different kinds. One concept for such a software production environment, called software factory, is under development in the EUREKA project ESF [1]. It aims at supporting all tasks in the production of software by providing a full coverage for the envisioned tool support. According to ESF these tools are integrated in a software factory that is composed of three types of basic building blocks:

1. User-interaction components, incorporating the FSE's interface to the user.
2. Service components, incorporating tools and data repository services in support of the software development process.
3. The software bus as a backbone for the interworking of user-interaction components and service components.

Software development does not only refer to a piece of source code in a particular programming language but to a large set of different kinds of documents, including requirements specifications, test reports, or user manuals. These documents are produced during different phases of the software development process using different tools with tool specific data management requirements and capabilities. In order to provide support for these different document types a software factory has to incorporate appropriate data management systems that may fill different purposes.

Besides conventional database management systems there is already a broad spectrum of object management systems (OMS's) and object-oriented database management systems available, either as commercial products or as research prototypes at different development stages (e.g. [2–11]). Different systems have their advantages for different applications. PCTE/OMS[2], for instance, is particularly useful for managing large objects like software modules and the like as every PCTE object comes along with 58 bytes of management information. GRAS[3] [13], on the other hand, is specifically suited for handling graph structures. Thus it is quite evident that a software development environment that aims at supporting the entire software development process would profit from the coexistence of both object management systems, especially if, for instance, graph-oriented methods are applied (e.g., Petri net approaches for some specifications).

The above requirements and the variety of existing OMS's make it obvious that object management system evolution is likely to continue before stabilization and standardization will occur. This process is permanently slowed down and disturbed by new competitors entering the race (e.g., IBM's Repository [14]). Furthermore, specific applications will always stimulate special solutions, resulting in nonstandard products that will be brought into their use as soon as they are available.

In order to homogenize data management in software development environments we present the object management machine (OMM) concept as an integration framework, for preexisting data management systems. An OMM enables the creation of uniform access patterns to different data management systems, including the query interface and transaction processing. The concept of the OMM is being developed in the framework of the ESF project with the ESF software bus[4] as a conceptual background. The software bus serves two purposes: it defines a conceptual model for the interoperation of components in a distributed software development environment and it provides a framework for the integration of software development components. It has to cope with the heterogeneity of user-interaction components and service components with different hardware platforms and with geographical distribution, for instance. The software bus is also supposed to enable the on-line attachment of new components ("plug-in" capability) and the detachment of others ("plug-off"), the management of services, and the management of users and groups of users.

The MUSE[5] multidatabase integrator has been demonstrated to be a suitable software bus instance [15]. Hence, we consider MUSE as appropriate for the implementation of the OMM concept as well.

The paper is organized as follows. We start by discussing the basics of the OMM concept. Then we investigate possible different types and degrees of OMS/OMM integration. The section closes with looking at OMM's as hierarchies of specific service components in a client/server model. In Part 2, we present the here relevant features of MUSE for the implementation of the OMM concept, i.e., the S-transaction concept and the MUSE architecture. On this basis we finally discuss single-level and multilevel integration of OMS's and OMM's, respectively, in MUSE.

2. The Object Management Machine (OMM) Concept

In order to avoid the coexistence of multiple object management system interfaces and concepts within a single software development environment, we propose the OMM concept as an integration framework for different object management systems followed by an investigation of different degrees of integration.

2.1. Fundamental Issues of an OMM

An OMM is meant to provide an integration framework for database management systems and object management systems, resulting in an open extensible OMM architecture as a data repository component in a complex system environment. The OMM defines a virtual machine that provides a uniform view on a number of different data management systems. An OMM encapsulates a set of object management systems, providing a client interface that includes a query language that encompasses transaction definitions. Figure 1 depicts the gross architecture of an OMM. The OMM consists of an object management machine integration framework (OMMIF) and a set of encapsulated OMS's.

The integration by means of the integration framework does not mean to provide the union of functionalities of the different encapsulated object management systems nor does it mean the redundant storing of information in different object management systems. It does mean the *standardization of user access patterns* to different OMM's.

An OMM is defined to encapsulate subordinate OMM's i.e., the OMM concept is recursively defined. Thus, an OMM provides an integration framework for OMS's and for OMM's Management Machines (see Figure 3).

In the following paragraphs we look briefly into the components of the OMM integration framework.

Client Interface	Object
OMM Body	Management Machine Integration Framework
Call Interface	
OMS₁ ... OMSₙ	Encapsulated OMS's

Object Management Machine

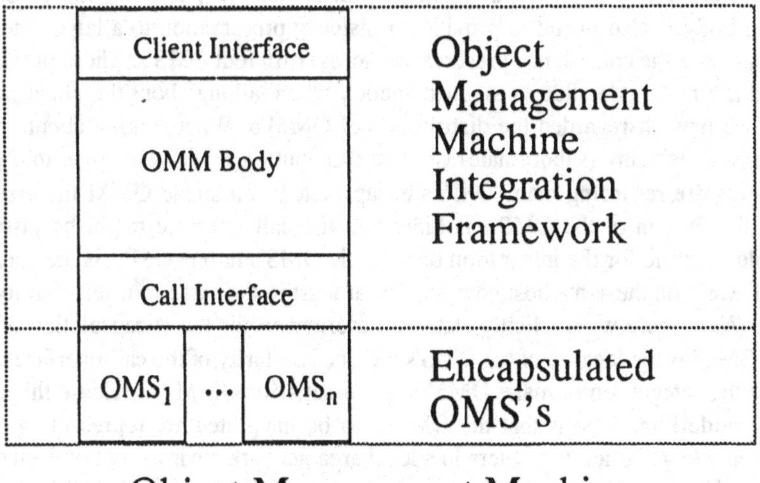

Figure 1. Architecture of an object management machine (OMM).

2.1.1. The Call Interface. The "call interface" is that part of the OMMIF that is specific for each object management system to be integrated. The view of an encapsulated OMS taken by the call interface is that of an abstract data type, providing an export interface with a set of functions that can be invoked by the OMM. For the execution of queries one may look at the OMS as a query language compiler or interpreter. If the OMS provides a procedural interface the implementation of the call interface is a straightforward matter: the encapsulation is achieved by using local or remote procedure calls, depending on the environment in which the OMM is implemented. If the OMS provides a language interface the call interface has to implement an adaptation to the respective OMS. The interpreter is implemented as an own process (e.g. Oracle's™ SQL*Plus™6) and the call interface then implements the invocation of OMS services by means of interprocess communication.

2.1.2. The OMM Body. In the simplest case the OMM encapsulates a single OMS. The body's task is then to adjust to access patterns for the access to the encapsulated OMS. The body maps the functions provided at the OMM Client Interface (OMMCI) into the corresponding functions of the encapsulated OMS. This mapping includes the preprocessing of parameters, postprocessing of results returned by the OMS and of the extension of the OMS's transaction mechanism towards the OMMCI.

If the OMM encapsulates many OMS's the just described functions of the body are complemented by a routing mechanism and—as a client can invoke operations that span multiple OMS's—a coordinator for distributed transaction processing. A detailed discussion of transaction processing problems is beyond the scope of this paper. In brief, we can say that the body functions are limited to commit coordination if the encapsulated OMS's support a commit protocol (e.g., 2-phase commit). Otherwise, the body integrates multiple transaction-based systems into a federated or multidatabase system (see [16]). Transaction processing becomes then a lot more complicated. The body has to cope not only with distributed transactions but with autonomous transactions [17] as well. The consequence is that the body is also meant to provide consistency preservation to a large extent since it is to supervise the consistency preservation across different OMS's. These problems are described a bit more detailed in the next section when talking about the client interface.

So far we have disregarded the distribution of OMM's. When talking about an OMM that encapsulates many (subordinate) OMM's distribution might also come into play. As long as we were regarding many OMS's encapsulated in a single OMM the assumption that the distribution of the OMS's is hidden in the call interface might be justified. A reasonable scenario for the integration of multiple OMS's in one OMM is the coexistence of these OMS's on the same host computer or at least in the same (cluster of a) local area network. (*Note*: here we implicitly state that a criterion for the encapsulation of OMS's into one OMM is the locality of the OMS's and the similarity of the call interfaces.) When regarding the integration of many OMM's into a superior OMM we release this assumption. The underlying idea is that the OMM's to be integrated are representing different environments (e.g., different clusters in a local area network environment or even different sites in a wide-area network environment). As a consequence an OMMIF's body itself must also incorporate an appropriate communication mechanism.

2.1.3. The OMM Client Interface (OMMCI). The client interface can play two different roles: it can be the called interface of a subordinate OMM to a superior one or it can be the interface of the top-level OMM. It is easy to understand that an OMM/OMM interface could differ from an OMM/User interface. For instance, two OMM's could use specific internal communication features and parameter passing mechanisms that depend on the actual system environment, whereas at the borderline between system and users or applications, respectively, a particular standard is required. However, for the sake of extensibility and maintainability we suggest the same kind of interface for all OMM's, independent of their role.

Regarding the interface in more detail we can easily identify several groups of functions that have to be provided in the OMMCI:

> Data management services
> Transaction processing services
> OMS integration services
> OMM integration services
> OMS and OMM management services

If we take distribution and multiuser processing into account we also include functions for authorization and authentication, encryption, and accounting.

In summary, we can say that an OMM has to provide the same groups of functions as an OMS and in addition integration and OMM and OMS management services. For the rest of this section we do not distinguish between OMS's and OMM's but regard them equally as components. In the sequel we concentrate on these added groups of functions for component management and for component integration.

2.2. Plug-In/Plug-Off of Components

Following the concepts of openness and extensibility the approach of OMM's seeks to support the dynamic incorporation and removal of new components to/from the OMM's that exist in a particular environment. Hence, the integration services provide functionality for the integration of new OMS's into an existing OMM as well as the integration of existing OMM's (on a peer level) into a superior OMM.

2.2.1. Component Integration Services. The term integration is meant to cover component installation as well as registration. A component must be physically available and executable on the platform under regard and the component must be made known to the rest of the system. If new component is integrated into an existing structure (e.g., a new OMS is added to an existing OMM) the name and the services provided by the new component must be registered at the existing structure in order to become accessible at the superior interface.

In a similar way the reverse operation, i.e., the removal of a component, must be supported. The OMM concept must provide means for dynamically removing services from the set of existing ones.

2.2.2. Component Management Services. With the set of component management services we refer to the maintenance of existing components. As typical management services we consider the creation and deletion of services provided by a component, the handling of user rights, accounting, licensing, usage monitoring, and the like.

2.3. Types and Degrees of Integration

A software development environment consists of a set of client components and OMM's can be integrated in a number of ways that also represent different degrees of integration.

As an initial case for the integration of tools we depict tools and their associated OMM's (Figure 2) that are subject to integration.

If the tools in Figure 2 use the same OMS (i.e., $OMS_1 = OMS_2$) according to [1], we call them horizontally integrated. Regarding now the OMM concept in its recursive form the situation can occur that the two tools use different OMS's as depicted in Figure 2 but that these OMS's are integrated in the same OMM (see Figure 3).

For the interface of a superior OMM we can again distinguish between two situations. On one hand, the integrated client interface (ICC) can mean the coexistence of the subordinate component interfaces in the integrated interface or the integrated interface represents an abstraction of the subordinate interfaces. We discuss these two alternatives in the following in more detail.

2.3.1. Coexistence. The coexistence type of OMS/OMM integration represents the lowest degree of integration. In the coexistence scenario the superior interface is the sum of the subordinate interfaces. If two subordinate components provide the same services they are renamed and offered as different services at the next higher-level interface. Thus, for the interface there is no difference to the scenario illustrated in Figure 3. This situation changes, however, with respect to the body of an OMM.

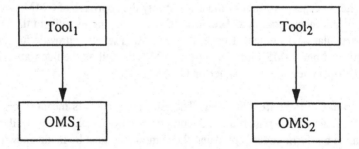

Figure 2. Non-integrated tools and OMSs.

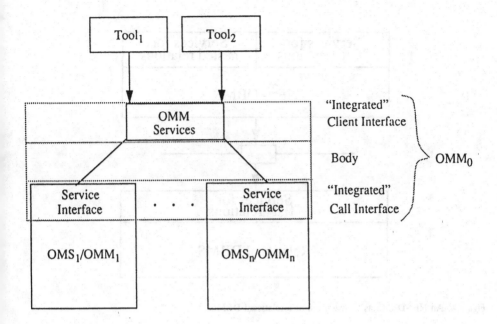

Figure 3. OMS/OMM integration.

The superior OMM integrates the encapsulated OMM/OMS's and thus provides the interface to the client of the superior OMM. It passes requests to the lower level components but does not provide an abstraction on the services. Services provided by the subordinate OMM/OMS's are executed as conventional transactions (c.f. [18]) against the respective OMS. Consistency constraints can only be enforced for individual OMS's. The role of the superior OMM is limited to providing a uniform 'look and feel' for the subordinate components.

2.3.2. *Extension*. A higher degree of integration is provided by an extension type OMM. The superior OMM does not simply pass through the services of the lower level. It extends this set through new, semantically richer services that make use of the lower level services. Figure 4 illustrates the relevance of this integration type for the practice.

A straightforward solution for the implementation of an NF^2 database system[7] is to place the NF^2 component on top of a relational database management system. The NF^2 component thus extends the set of data management services for flat relations, provided by the conventional database system, through additional services for the management of nested relations. As the NF^2 system also offers the lower level services, the newly added services can be regarded as an extension.

2.3.3. *Abstraction*. In contrast to the extension approach the abstraction, provided at the superior OMM interface, is meant to be a completely new interface on the basis of the encapsulating components. The newly defined services then work across individual OMM/OMS boundaries, i.e., they can use subservices of different lower-level OMM/OMS's.

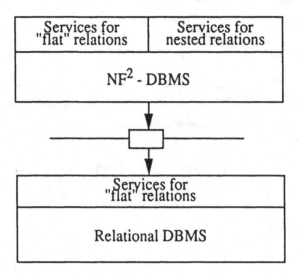

Figure 4. An NF^2-DBMS as an extension of a relational DBMS.

Each service provided at the superior OMM interface is performed as well as a transaction. To support transactions at that level the OMM provides transaction processing functions that embed the transaction processing capabilities of the subordinate OMM/OMS's. That enables the invocation of transaction-based services across OMS and/or OMM boundaries. Thus, it is now also possible to define consistency constraints across a number of integrated OMS's and OMM's. It is up to the body of the superior OMM to care for the preservation of these consistency constraints.

The consistency constraints could either be static or dynamic. The static consistency constraints are hard coded in the bodies of the superior OMM's by means of predefined transactions, i.e., the types and paths of interactions between a superior OMM and its subordinate components are predefined. The consistency is user defined by the transaction designer. For the dynamic case the knowledge about consistency across components is incorporated in ad hoc transactions. Hence, consistency is user defined by the designer of the ad hoc transactions.

If the subordinate components support commit protocols for distributed transaction processing, the top-level OMM can take the role of a commit coordinator in order to control the proper termination of transactions that span multiple components [19]. On the other hand, i.e., if the components do not support commit protocols but run conventional transactions (c.f. [18]), there is no way for guaranteeing global consistency [20]. A practical example for an abstraction-type OMM is IBM's Repository Manager [21].

The MVS-operating system based repository manager implementation consists of two levels. On the lower level there are the base systems for data management, i.e., the DB2 relational database management system[8] and the MVS file system. Each of the lower-level components provides a specific set of data management services (In the context of the preceding discussion we also regard the file system as an OMS (see Figure 5).

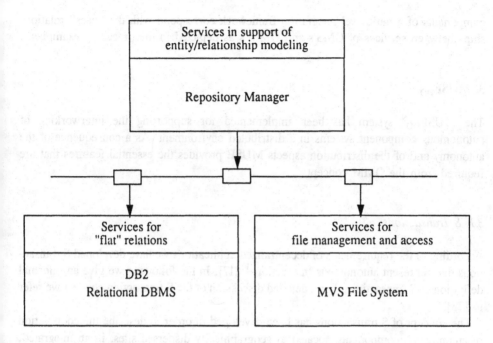

Figure 5. The IBM repository manager as an abstraction of DB2 and the MVS file system.

The two components are integrated into the repository manager, which represents the upper level. The repository manager uses the services of the lower level for the implementation of its own service interface that is designed for supporting entity/relationship modeling. Thus, the repository manager implements an abstraction-type OMM. The base-level services are hidden from the upper-level client. Instead, the upper level provides semantically richer services.

2.4. Modeling OMM's as Hierarchies of Service Components

As described in the Introduction, a software factory basically consists of a set of peer service components. Typical examples for a service component in the context of this paper are OMS's and OMM's. Regarding now the recursive definition of OMM's and the preceding examples, the inclusion of the OMM concept in the framework of the ESF reference architecture for a software factory implies a revision or refinement of the gross architecture. An extension towards the hierarchical ordering of service components in general is discussed in [22]. The ordering of service components on a peer level as described in the beginning of this paper is called single-level integration. The hierarchical ordering of components, which is important for the OMM concept, is referred to as multilevel integration framework. The consequence of the multilevel integration is the demand for enabling a service component to act as a client of a subordinate service component, i.e., a service component does not only need an export interface for the services provided by itself but also an import interface to subordinate service components. The hierarchical call relationships between components of a multilevel integration framework correspond with the "uses" relationships between services of OMS's and OMM's as depicted in the preceding examples.

3. MUSE$_{DO}$

The MUSE$_{DO}$[9] system has been implemented for supporting the interworking of autonomous component systems in a distributed environment. As a consequence of the autonomy and of the distribution aspects MUSE provides the essential features that are required from the OMM concept.

3.1. S Transactions

According to the requirements of decentralized applications we have developed S transactions that represent autonomous transactions[10] [17]. In the following we give an informal definition of S transactions. For a detailed discussion of the S transaction concept we refer to [23].

The concept of S transactions has been developed in order to describe the cooperation of autonomous components, located to geographically dispersed sites, in an integrated, cooperative system. The underlying system model is that of a set of cooperating peer components. The interrelationships between these components are dynamically defined within S transaction type definitions, i.e., there is no strict static hierarchy.

An S transaction is recursively defined. It (i.e., the entire or global S transaction) consists of a top-level S transaction that is composed of a set of subordinate S transactions and local transactions (LT's). The local transactions interface to the applications that are allocated to the local sites. Hence, by definition, S transactions are multilevel transactions. A top-level S transaction is the parent node for a set of subordinate S transactions that are initiated at logically different sites. (Normally, these sites are geographically dispersed.) Any S transaction can request services from an application system at the site it is allocated to (referred to as a local site). These services are provided by the local site as transactions and hence are called local transactions. Local transactions are self-contained, conventional transactions, i.e., they are executed as transactions providing atomicity, consistency, isolation, and durability (c.f. [18]). Consequently they commit prior to the termination of their parent S transactions.

The implementation of local transactions is in the responsibility of the local sites (due to their autonomy). Hence, implementations of the same local transaction may differ from site to site. Its semantics, however, must be the same at each site. A local transaction is executed under the control of the local site and the site is responsible for the recovery of the failing transaction. Thus, we preserve the local site's execution autonomy as the local transaction execution control is beyond the scope of the S transaction that requests the local transaction. In general, recovery from failure during the execution of a local transaction is performed by means of conventional UNDO recovery techniques, i.e., backward recovery [18].

Recovery of S transactions is based on compensation [24]. For any component S-transaction ST and for any local transaction LT we require the existence of compensating transactions ST's and LT's, respectively. An S transaction type is described in the S transaction definition language, STDL. As the features of STDL are of no concern for the following discussion we refer the interested reader to [25] or [26] for a detailed description of the language.

3.2. MUSE Site Architecture

The MUSE sites (in the following simply referred to as sites) have a uniform architecture that reflects the layered architecture of the entire system. The design of the site architecture is based on the principles of strict modularity, and hierarchy. In particular, the architecture is composed of a set of modules. Each module represents an abstract data type, incorporating a data structure and corresponding operations. At the interface of a module only the exported functions are visible. The relations between modules are "uses"-relations that define a hierarchy, leading to an acyclic graph with directed edges in a graphical representation.

As depicted in Figure 6 the MUSE integration layer only interfaces to the local application system. That means the local site fully preserves its autonomy regarding design, communication, and execution (c.f. [23]). In order to be able to be integrated into the MUSE system a site has to fulfill the following requirements:

1. Operations at the local site are performed as conventional transactions [18], guaranteeing atomicity, consistency, isolation, and durability for these operations.
2. Sites integrated into MUSE communicate exclusively with each other via the mechanisms provided by MUSE; we assume that sites do not circumvent the MUSE-control mechanisms by directly communicating with each other.
3. A local site does not distinguish between transactions issued by MUSE and those issued by local users via the local interface.

These design constraints are reflected in the MUSE architecture as well as in the underlying concept of S transactions. Figure 6 illustrates the gross architecture of a MUSE site. The main components are briefly discussed as follows.

The user interaction layer of the site architecture consists of the following modules. The Canned__Transaction__Definition module (CT__Def) supports the definition of new predefined S transactions, extending the set of standard services provided by MUSE. The newly defined S transaction types are specified in STDL and are stored in a library, i.e., in the Canned__Transactions__Module (CTM).

The Application__User__Functions module (AUF) supports the execution of predefined S transactions. The AUF module exports a set of functions for the initiation, abort, status supervision, and result handling of S transactions. It can either interface to an interactive application interface or the exported functions can directly be imported by an application program.

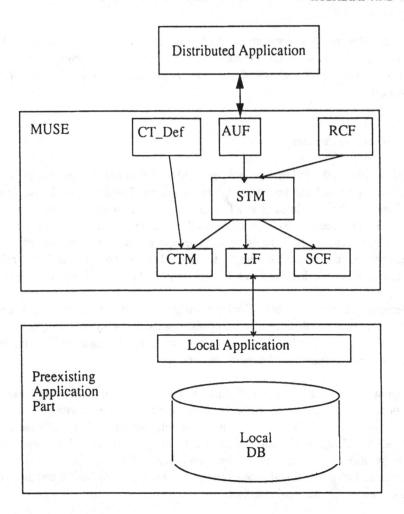

Figure 6. MUSE site architecture.

The S transaction management STM controls the execution of S transactions, i.e., it coordinates the execution of S transactions and local transactions. All actions of the S transaction management are performed as conventional transactions, i.e., they are robust against system failures. The S transaction management also provides a log-based recovery mechanism for S transactions. The execution plans of the predefined S transactions are passed to the S transaction management (STM) for execution. The STM interprets the S transaction execution plans, i.e., the STDL Interpreter within the STM interprets the STDL scripts. Requests for subordinate S transactions or local transactions are submitted to the Send_Control_ Functions module (SCF) or to the Local_Functions module (LF). Results, acknowledgments, and abort requests are also transferred to remote sites via SCF.

The STM's log module records all incoming and outgoing messages, the initiation and termination of S transactions. All message transfers and all local function invocations within an S transaction at one site are recorded in the log module. This information is needed for recovery from site failures or for compensation of S transactions.

The SCF interfaces the site to the message handling system. It transforms the requests submitted by the STM into the messages that are passed on to the message handling system for sending to remote sites. The Receive_Control_Functions module (RCF) receives messages from remote sites and transforms them into corresponding function calls to the STM.

Finally, the Local_Functions module (LF) is MUSE's interface to the local site database system. The requests for operations on the local database that are defined in the S transaction execution plans are passed from the STM to the local database via LF.

A MUSE site is implemented in C($>$ 100,000 lines of code) as a set of communicating processes, running on SUN/3, SUN/4, and VAX under SUN OS 3.5 and later and VMS, respectively. As mentioned earlier, all operations within MUSE are performed as conventional transactions for reliability reasons and in order to be able to provide an unconventional transaction mechanism on top of components that provide their own conventional transaction mechanism. In order to reduce our implementation work we originally used a relational DBMS as a persistent storage for MUSE internal data and for S transaction data. The relations were shared by several processes and the DBMS provided for synchronization. As the performance of the system was not acceptable we reimplemented parts of the system, keeping now the data structures in main memory and using module specific mechanisms for concurrency control and recovery. The resulting performance improvements are up to two orders of magnitude (i.e., a factor of 100) reducing execution times from minutes to seconds for distributed applications.

In order to support local area and wide area network communication the communication subsystem integrates local communication by means of UNIX domain sockets and communication by means of the TCP/IP protocol for local and wide area networks. In an earlier version we also provided for X.400.

3.2.1. Service Provision in MUSE. The applicability of the S transaction concept will be illustrated now as in [27]. The following example explains the interworking of different OMS's as an S transaction with the aid of the MUSE system.

Let us assume that a software developer D1 with a private OMS1 at site S1 has finished the specification of a software module. He wants to transfer this partial result from his OMS to OMS2 of a developer D2 at a site S2. We further assume that S1 and S2 run instances of different OMS types. Finally, there is a site S3 that maintains a converter for the conversion of OMS1 objects into those of OMS2.

The transfer is then performed in the following steps:
1. Transfer of the intermediate result from OMS1 to the converter at S3.
2. Message from S1 to S2, indicating the transfer of the result object via S3
3. Transfer of the converted result object from S3 into OMS2 at S2.

MUSE provides services as S transactions, provided at the AUF interface. Each S transaction type, as defined and stored in the CTM module, represents a service class. An instantiation of an S-transaction type, i.e., an S transaction, corresponds to a service. In order to provide a service an S transaction normally uses local transactions, i.e., services provided by the local application component (which could be data repository services as well), and maybe services from remote sites, resulting in the invocation of subordinate S transactions.

The object conversion and transfer service as outlined in the above example is provided as follows. Developer D1 requests a transfer service from MUSE site S1, using the MUSE AUF interface. That triggers the initiation of an S transaction ST1 at the STM of S1. ST1 requests a local service from S1 in order to check out the desired object. This local service is performed as a local function, provided by the LF module of S1, that encapsulates the checkout function, provided by OMS1. Furthermore, ST1 submits a request (2) through the SCF module to S2 in order to initiate a subordinate S transaction ST2 at MUSE site S2.

The RCF module at S2 eventually receives the request and triggers the initiation of the requested S transaction type at its local STM. The STM fetches the corresponding S transaction execution plan from its CTM module and activates the appropriate part according to the actual parameters that were passed on from the RCF as ST2. In our particular example ST2 is set to "waiting" for the object that is to be sent by S3.

Then, in the same way, ST1 requests a subordinate S transaction ST3 from the converter site S3. As just described for ST2 S transaction ST3 is initiated at S3. ST3 incorporates the transfer (1), a request for a local service at S3 that implements the conversion, and the submission of a message from S3 to S2 in which the converted result is passed on to the previously initiated ST2 (3). According to this execution plan the STM at S3 performs the corresponding operations.

The converted result is received by the RCF at S2. One parameter of the message is the identification of the previously initiated S transaction ST2. Upon receipt of the result from site S3, ST2 is reactivated. It performs a local function by which the result is checked in into OMS2, i.e., the local function of the LF module at S2 encapsulates the checkin function provided by OMS2.

4. MUSE as a Framework for OMM's

When comparing the requirements of the OMM integration framework with the MUSE inherent concepts and with the way how MUSE provides services, some resemblances are quite evident. MUSE provides for communication between components (message passing as well as broadcasting and multicasting) and supports transaction management across components as required by an OMM. MUSE's S transactions enable the specification of conventional distributed transactions as well as the specification of autonomous transactions and MUSE allows these transaction types to coexist within the same environment [28]. These facilities of MUSE are extensively used for supporting different types of OMS/OMM integration, which is discussed next.

Due to the recursive definition of the OMM concept two levels of integration, i.e., single-level and multilevel integration, can apply to the OMM concept. We have to investigate how these integrations are supported in MUSE described in Section 4.1.2. There, we start with a discussion of single-level OMM's and continue with multilevel OMM's, i.e., OMM's that encapsulate subordinate OMM's. Finally, we discuss the problem of dynamic component integration in MUSE.

4.1. Support of OMS/OMM Integration Types

In Section 2 we discussed the OMM demand for two different types of integration, i.e., the coexistence of components and what we called abstraction–the integration of components into a component that provides higher service qualities. In the following paragraphs, we briefly sketch how these integration types can be implemented in MUSE.

4.1.1. Coexistence. Disregarding the different levels of integration that are discussed later we can regard, without loss of generality, the coexistence of two OMS's within a single MUSE instance. Obviously, the OMS's have to interface with the LF component of the MUSE instance, i.e., logically we divide the set of local functions of the MUSE instance into two disjoint subsets, one for each OMS. Each local function maps exactly into a function that is provided by the related OMS.

Next step, we define a corresponding set of S transactions that are provided to the user at the AUF interface. Each S transaction contains only one local function call and the S transaction has the same parameters as the local function, i.e., we extend the de facto local function interface to the user. Thus, we have put MUSE on top of the two OMS's under regard and MUSE defines the same 'look and feel' for their interfaces. If any two OMS's/OMM's export the same services to the superior OMM the ambiguity is resolved through renaming.

Note, that the coexistence-type OMM is not implemented as a specific service component that interfaces to the MUSE system. Instead, the coexistence OMM materialized as a corresponding set of S transaction types that are stored in the CTM modules of the MUSE instances. In other words, the body of a coexistence OMM is empty (c.f. Figure 3). The services provided by the lower-level components are passed on as S transaction types in the superior-level client interface.

As an example for a coexistence-type OMM we present in the following the interface of the Oracle relational DBMS that has been integrated into the MUSE system. At the level of local functions the encapsulated Oracle component provides the following set of functions:

1. connect, disconnect for establishing the link between a user and a database, taking the user identification and the password as parameters.
2. sql_statement with an SQL string (data definition statement as well as data manipulation statement) as input parameter and the name of a resultfile (for select statements) as output parameter.
3. sql_statement_c, which connects to the database, executes the statement, given as input parameter, and disconnects.
4. sql_file that has a filename as input parameter where the file contains a sequence of SQL statements, and a result filename as output parameter. The result file then contains the concatenated set of results correlating to the select statements in the input file.

These functions can be used for interoperation with Oracle through pipes or via system call. In addition we provide the same set of functions for communicating via the descriptor area, provided by Oracle (and in a similar way by other relational database systems like DB2, Ingres, or Informix, for instance). The advantage of this solution is that results of a select are not returned as a simple string as in the previous approach, but the results are returned as structures that can be immediately used for further operations whereas the result string can only be displayed or needs interpretation (by means of parsing) for further automatic processing.

For the coexistence category of integration we provide the just described functions as S transaction services at the MUSE interface where the body of the S transaction definition simply consists of the function call to the LF interface. We can do that for an object-oriented system like PCTE/OMS in a very similar way as for Oracle. Of course, we can connect other relational DBMS's with an SQL interface in the same way as Oracle, particularly when they also provide a descriptor area for communication.

4.1.2. Extension. In contrast to the coexistence type, an extension-type OMM does not only pass through the services of lower-level components but also provides additional functionality. The place to add functionality in a MUSE instance is at the local functions (LF) interface. Hence, the body of the extension type OMM is implemented as a set of local functions, accessible through MUSE's LF interface.

The service interface of the extension OMM consists of a subset of simple S transaction types that provide direct access to the lower level services and of a subset of complex S transaction types that incorporate the additional functionality provided by the superior OMM. The simple S transaction types of the first subset simply consist of a call to the lower-level service. The complex S transaction types are composed of local function calls to the extension OMM body and of service calls to subordinate components.

An example for an extension-type OMM is the previously mentioned NF^2 database system if it is implemented on top of a conventional relational DBMS. In that case we can offer the relational DBMS services at the MUSE interface in the same way as described in the preceding section. In addition we can provide NF^2 services that extend the simple relational ones as the following example illustrates.

Assume that a company has several departments and a department has several members. In terms of nested relations that can be represented by a company relation with the company name and the departments as attributes. The company name is an atomic attribute (i.e., a string) while the department is a relation again, consisting of the department name and the members where a member is another relation, consisting of name, address, and so forth.

In an NF^2 system this scenario can be defined as a single NF^2 relation and we can use an extended SQL for the manipulation of such NF^2 relations. The NF^2 component internally maps the NF^2 relation into a set of conventional relations managed by the conventional DBMS. The complex attributes of the company relation are implemented as simple relations that get in addition the company name attribute as a link attribute in order to represent the 1:n relationship between company name and department. The member relation in turn inherits the department name and the company name as link attributes to represent the 1:n relationship between member and department. The names of the link attributes are automatically generated by the NF^2 component.

The NF^2 component is integrated as a new component at local function level in MUSE. The NF^2 interface looks the same as the relational one except that the input strings are now extended SQL (NF^2 SQL) and the result of an NF^2 function is not the final result but the decomposition of the NF^2 query into corresponding SQL queries, which are then issued against the relational system, using its local function interface. Regarding the structure of an S transaction for the extension part, it does not contain a single local-function call, but it does contain at least one call to the NF^2 component and a subsequent call to the relational DBMS component using the output of the NF^2 part as an input for the relational part.

A client can now operate on the relational DBMS on simple relations using the corresponding services provided at the MUSE interface or the NF^2 services as an extension of the simple relational services.

4.1.3. Abstraction. According to the definition of abstraction type OMM's in Section 2.2.3 the abstraction OMM encapsulates the services of subordinate components and provides higher quality services. From the implementation point of view, the abstraction OMM differs from the extension OMM insofar as the abstraction OMM does not pass through services of subordinate components at all. It provided only newly defined services. Their implementation is the same as for the additional services of an extension OMM, i.e., they are implemented in the abstraction OMM body as a set of local functions.

As an example for an abstraction type OMM we consider a media DBMS as an example that internally uses a relational system for storing the registration data of media objects (e.g., image size, encoding format, sound sampling rate, date of creation, ownership) and the file system for storing the bit streams that contain the real media object (e.g., image bitmap, digitized sound recording.)

At the client interface the media OMM provides service for the management of media objects that are internally decomposed into subordinate services that are provided by the relational DBMS and/or by the file system component. The decomposition, however, is hidden to the OMM client.

A representative for such an abstraction OMM is a multimedia DBMS that has been developed at the Naval Postgraduate School, Monterey, CA [29,30]. At the MUSE-interface level, a set of media object related services is offered. The media component is integrated at the local-functions level as described for the extension OMM. The media component decomposes queries as described for the NF^2 part above and issues the subqueries against the subordinate systems (i.e., Oracle and/or the file system).

4.2. Support of Different OMS/OMM Integration Levels

Next to the types of integration the problem of integration levels has been discussed for OMM's. In this section we present appropriate solutions for the implementation of integration levels in MUSE.

4.2.1. Single-Level Integration. When regarding the MUSE architecture in Figure 6 MUSE's approach toward single-level integration is obvious: the preexisting application part in Figure 7 is a representative of a set of integrated OMM's. This means that the LF module has to implement the connection between MUSE and the application components, i.e., the OMM's in this particular situation.

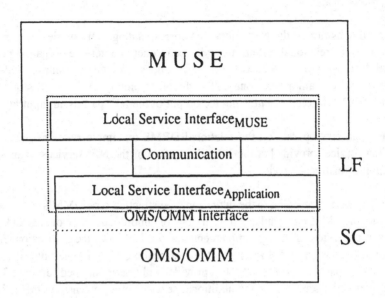

Figure 7. Refinement of MUSE's local functions (LF) component.

Figure 7 illustrates a refined view of MUSE's LF component. The LF module actually consists of three basic parts: the local service interface within MUSE, the local interface that establishes the connection between the application program and MUSE, and a communication channel between the two local service interface parts. Within a single-level integration framework, the role of MUSE is shown in Figure 8.

Figure 8 allows at least two different interpretations: either the three boxes in Figure 8 form a part of a single MUSE instance or each small box represents another MUSE instance. If a single MUSE instance is used for the integration (Figure 9 (a)), the user interaction component (UIC) interfaces to the AUF module of the MUSE instance, represented through the small box in the middle of the figure and the service components connect to the LF component, which is split into two parts, one for each service component. According to this interpretation the UIC uses S transactions that are provided by MUSE at the AUF interface. These S transactions contain local transaction calls that are submitted to the service components.

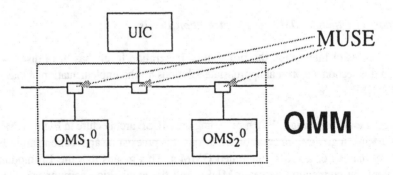

Figure 8. The role of MUSE in a single-level integration framework.

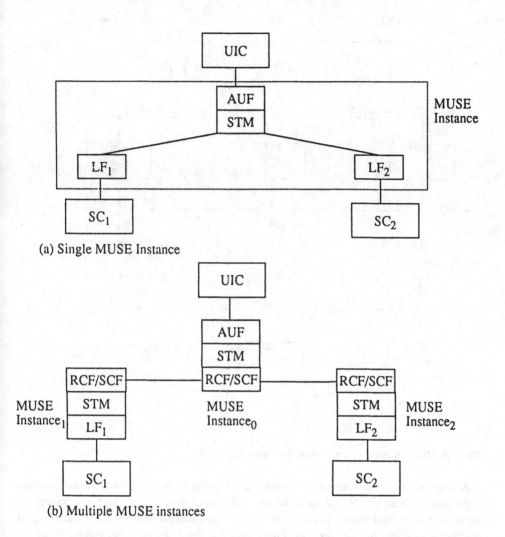

(a) Single MUSE Instance

(b) Multiple MUSE instances

Figure 9. Single-level service component integeration in MUSE.

An alternative solution is the use of multiple MUSE instances, one for each small box in figure 9(b). In that case the UIC initiates a (root) S transaction at the MUSE instance it is attached to and this root transaction initiates subordinate S transactions at the MUSE instances where the service components are connected to. The services provided by the service components are still accessible through the LF components of the MUSE instances. Thus, with respect to the quality of services the second interpretation or solution is not better than the first one.

4.2.2. Multilevel Server Integration. The basic motivation for the multilevel integration is the demand for enabling a service component to act as a client of a subordinate service component (Figure 10). Then, a service component does not only need an export interface for the services provided by itself but also an import interface to subordinate service components.

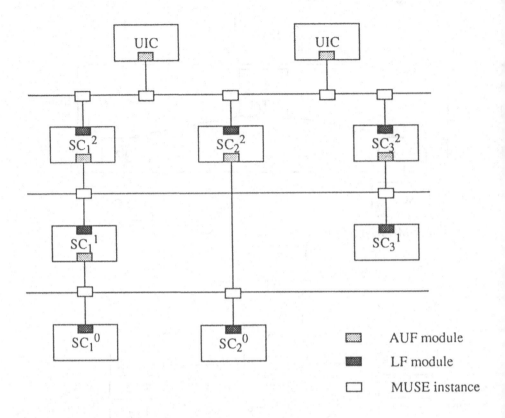

Figure 10. MUSE instances in a multi-level integration framework.

A solution has already been discussed in the preceding section: the encapsulation of each service component in a MUSE instance where the services of each service component are accessible as S transactions to all other service components. That means a flattening of the hierarchical structure and the loss of the statically defined "users" relationships. However, the "users" relationships are not completely lost but the static definition is replaced by a dynamic one. The UIC get only access to the S transactions that are exported from the service components that are logically allocated to the top level of the service component hierarchy and the static "uses" relationships are encoded in these S transactions. Then the logical view of the entire system is still the same, whereas the implementation differs. The major advantage of this solution is that all interactions between components are defined as S transactions. Hence, the MUSE system is able to enforce consistency constraints even across level boundaries.

4.3. Component Integration

An important requirement of the OMM concept is the demand for the capability of dynamic integration and detachment of components. An exhaustive discussion of MUSE's support in that respect is beyond the scope of this paper and can be found in [31]. Instead, we restrict ourselves to a brief description of the major steps.

For the sake of simplicity we start with the integration on the basis of a single-level integration as depicted in Figure 9(a). The integration of a new component basically means the extension of the set of local functions. From the implementation point of view that means that the list of local services maintained in the Local Service Interface$_{Application}$ (see Figure 7), is extended by the set of functions that is exported from the new component. In order to make these newly added services accessible to the entire system they have to be integrated into S transactions. In the simplest case, we follow the coexistence approach and export the local functions as S transactions. This integration step can be performed automatically. Regarding the abstraction approach it is easy to understand that the automatic integration of new local functions into existing, complex S transactions can hardly be achieved. This is also true for the creation of new abstract services.

If we consider a single-level integration according to Figure 9(b) the first steps are basically the same as just described. A new MUSE instance has to be generated and the component services are integrated into the Local Services Interface$_{Application}$ according to the above schema. In a further step, however, the newly created S transactions have to be made known to the superior MUSE instance. This is achieved through specifically defined S transactions that form an integral part of each MUSE instance. By means of these S transactions the newly defined S transactions are shipped to remote sites and are inserted into their service catalogs, maintained in the CTM module.

The integration of new components in a multilevel component hierarchy is basically the same. If the hierarchy is implemented as illustrated in Figure 10 the entire process has to be performed manually. If the hierarchy is dynamically created at least parts of the integration might be performed automatically as described for the single-level integration above. For the detachment of components the above-described procedures have to be reversed.

5. Conclusion

In this paper we discuss the concept of object management machines (OMM's) as an integration framework for different coexisting object management machines within a single software development environment in the context of the ESF project. The ESF Software Bus provides the conceptual basis for the interworking of OMS's and OMM's as specific service components.

An OMM is a hierarchy of (subordinate) OMM's and OMS's. Regarding the integrative power of a superior OMM we distinguish between three types of integration: coexistence, extension, and abstraction.

Coexistence describes a weaker degree of integration than extension or abstraction. An OMM that supports the coexistence of subordinate components provides a broad service interface that is the sum of the underlying component interfaces. The services, executed as a conventional transaction affect only a single OMS. The main purpose of the OMM/OMS hierarchy is to provide a homogenized access to different OMS's.

Extension means that the services provided by subordinate components are not only passed through by the superior OMM but that the superior OMM provides additional services that use the services exported from the underlying components. Thus, an extension OMM provides a higher-level interface, compared to a coexistence OMM.

Abstraction refers to a furthergoing approach. The services that are provided by an OMM on a higher level are constructed from imported services but do not represent a one-to-one mapping as in the coexistence approach. A higher-level service can span several subordinate components. As a consequence, the integrating OMM is an instance where consistency constraints can be defined that stretch over multiple OMS's.

For turning the conceptual model of OMM's into an implementation we use the $MUSE_{DO}$ system. It features the S-transaction concept, a powerful and flexible control mechanism that enables the coexistence of conventional distributed transactions and autonomous transactions. This flexibility is strongly demanded in order to enable the integration of different (preexisting) OMS's into OMM's and the interworking of different OMM's within the same software factory environment. The implementation of the different types and levels of component integration are as well described as the dynamic integration and detachment of components in MUSE.

Right now, MUSE is used as a vehicle for the evaluation of single-level integration regarding coexistence and abstraction of OMM interfaces. In the next step we extend our implementation towards multilevel integration.

Acknowledgments

The authors are indebted to Wolfgang Deiters and Volker Gruhn for the fruitful discussions and comments on earlier versions of this paper.

References

1. W. Schaefer and H. Weber, "The ESF profile," in *Handbook of Computer Aided Software Engineering*. Van Nostrand: New York, 1990.
2. M. Ahlsen et al, "OPAL–An object-based system for application development," *IEEE Database Eng.* vol. 8, no. 4, pp. 000–000, 1985.
3. F. Bancilhon et.al. "The design and implementation of O2, an object-oriented database system," in K. R. Dittrich, ed., "Advances in object-oriented database systems," *Proc. 2nd Int. Workshop Object-Oriented Database Syst. LNCS, Band 334*. Springer-Verlag: New York, 1988.
4. A. Bjoernerstedt and S. Britts, "AVANCE–An object management system," in *Proc. OOPSLA'88, ACM SIGPLAN N* vol. 23, no. 11, pp. 000–000, 1988.
5. K. R. Dittrich, W. Gotthard, P. C. Lockemann, "DAMOKLES–A database system for software engineering environments," in R. Conradi, T. M. Didriksen, D. H. Wanvik, ed., *Proc. Int. Workshop Advanced Programming Environments, LNCS, Band 244*. Springer-Verlag: New York, 1986.
6. C. Damon, "VBASE object-oriented database system," *ACM S R.* vol. 17, no. 2, pp. 000–000, 1988.
7. D. H. Fishman, et. a. "IRIS: An object-oriented database management system, *ACM TOIS*, vol. 5, no. 1, pp. 216–226, 1987.
8. W. Kim, et al. "Features of the ORION object-oriented database," in W. Kim, and H. L. Lochovsky, *Object-oriented concepts, databases, and applications*. ACM Press, Addison-Wesley: Reading, MA. 1989.

9. D. J. Moore, et al., "Vishnu: An object oriented database management system supporting software engineering," in *Proc. 12th Computer Software Appl. Conf.* (COMPSAC'88), Chicago, IL, 1988.

10. D. J. Maier, J. Stein, A. Otis, and A. Purdy, "Development of an object-oriented DBMS," in *Proc. OOPSLA 1986, ACM SIGPLAN Notices* vol. 21, no. 11, pp. 472–482, December 1986.

11. M. Stonebraker, and L. A. Rowe, "The design of postgres," in *Proc. Int. Conf. Management Data, ACM SIGMOD R.* vol. 15, no. 2, pp. 340–355, 1986.

12. F. Gallo, R. Minot, and I. Thomas, "The object management system of PCTE as a software engineering database management system," *ACM S N* vol. 22, no. 1, pp. 000–000, 1987.

13. C. Lewerenz and A. Schuerr, "GRAS, A management system for graph-like documents," in *Proc. 3rd Int. Conf. Data and Knowledge Bases.* Morgan Kaufmann, Los Altos, CA, 1988.

14. V. J. Mercurio, B. F. Meyers, A. M. Nisbet, and G. Radin, Description of AD/Cycle in *IBM Sys.* vol. 29, no. 2, pp. 170–188, 1990.

15. B. Holtkamp, "An ESF software bus instance," September 1990 (submitted for publication).

16. A. P. Sheth and J. A. Larson, "Federated database systems for managing distributed, heterogeneous, and autonomous databases," *ACM Computing Surveys* vol. 22, no. 3, pp. 183–236, September 1990.

17. International Standardization Organization, "Open systems interconnection–Distributed transaction processing part 1: Model," ISO Draft Proposal 10026-1, 1988.

18. J. N. Gray, "Notes on database operating systems," in R. Bayer, R. Graham, and G. Seegmüller, ed., *Lecture Notes in Computer Science 60, Operating Systems–An Advanced Course* (S.393–481). Springer, New York, 1978.

19. S. Ceri and G. Pelagatti, *Distributed Databases, Principles and Systems.* McGraw-Hill: New York, 1984.

20. Y. Breitbart, A. Silberschatz, and G. R. Thompson, *Trans. Management Issues Autonomous Heterogeneous DBMS,* in *Proc. Workshop Heterogeneous Database Sys.,* Evanston (Ill.), December 1989.

21. M. J. Sawaga, 'Repository Manager techniques,' *IBM Sys. J.* vol. 29, no. 2, pp. 209–227, 1990.

22. R. Adomeit, K. Lichtinghagen, B. Holtkamp, and H. Weber, "ESF factory support environment: Architectural refinements and alternatives," Internal Memorandum, Computer Science Department/Software Technology, University of Dortmund, July 1990.

23. F. Eliassen, J. Veijalainen, and B. Holtkamp, "The S-transaction model," in *Database Transaction Models for Advanced Applications''*. A. K. Elmagarmid, ed., Morgan Kaufmann, Los Altos, CA, 1991.

24. J. N. Gray, "The transaction concept: Virtues and limitations," *Proc. 7th VLDB Conf.,* pp. 144–154, 1981.

25. M. Hallmann and B. Holtkamp, "STLD: A definition language for semantic transactions," in *Proc. GI-Conf. Databases Software Eng.* Dortmund, November 1987.

26. SWIFT, University of Dortmund, "S-Transactions," MAP Project 761B Multidatabase Services on ISO/OSI Networks for Transnational Accounting, Deliverable No. 6, University of Dortmund, eds., December 1988.

27. B. Holtkamp, "Preserving autonomy in a heterogeneous multidatabase system," in *Proc. 12th Int. Computer Software Appl. Conf.* (COMP-SAC'88), Chicago, IL, October 1988.

28. B. Holtkamp, D. K. Hsiao, and V. Y. Lum, "Heterogeneous database systems: MUSE—Levels of integration," in *Proc. Workshop Heterogeneous Database Sys.,* Evanston, Il, December 1989.

29. B. Holtkamp, V. Y. Lum, and N. C. Rowe, "DEMOM—A description-based media object data model," in *Proc. 14th Annual Int. Computer Software Appl. Conf. (COMP-SAX'90),* Chicago, (Il), October 90.

30. B. Holtkamp, and V. Y. Lum, "Integration of alphanumeric and media data," internal memorandum no. 48, Computer Science Department/Software Technology, University of Dortmund, July 1990.

31. B. Holtkamp, and K. Lichtinghagen, "Service component integration in MUSE," internal memorandum, Computer Science Department/Software Technology, University of Dortmund (in preparation).

Journal of Systems Integration, 1, 391–409 (1991)

An Integrated Automatic Test Data Generation System

A. JEFFERSON OFFUTT
Department of Computer Science, Clemson University, Clemson, SC 29634

(Received July 30, 1990; Revised April 16, 1991)

Abstract. The Godzilla automatic test data generator is an integrated collection of tools that implements a relatively new test data generation method—constraint-based testing—that is based on mutation analysis. Constraint-based testing integrates mutation analysis with several other testing techniques, including statement coverage, branch coverage, domain perturbation, and symbolic evaluation. Because Godzilla uses a rule-based approach to generate test data, it is easily extendible to allow new testing techniques to be integrated into the current system. This article describes the system that has been built to implement constraint-based testing. Godzilla's design emphasizes orthogonality and modularity, allowing relatively easy extensions. Godzilla's internal structure and algorithms are described with emphasis on internal structures of the system and the engineering problems that were solved during the implementation.

Key Words: constraints, fault-based testing, mutation testing, software testing, test data generation, unit testing

1. Overview

We consider a program *unit* to be a subroutine, function, or (relatively) small collection of related subroutines and functions. In this article, program units are sometimes referred to as programs when the distinction is unimportant. Unit testing, therefore, is concerned with testing small components of programs, as opposed to integration, system, or acceptance testing, which are concerned with larger components. Although testing has been shown to be more effective at finding faults at the unit level, and fixing faults is less espensive when faults are detected during unit testing, the majority of testing of practical software is done at the integration or the system level [9, 12]. Unit testing is typically done by programmers who are poorly trained and equipped to apply structured testing strategies. Part of the difficulty with applying the available structured techniques for unit testing is that large software systems typically have hundreds or thousands of program units. To overcome this difficulty, unit testing must be automated, and this article describes a research system that automates much of unit testing by generating unit-level test data automatically. We hope that tests of large systems can be composed from tests of smaller subsystems and functions if the system structure admits, e.g., a hierarchical decomposition.

Another problem is that although several techniques have been developed that have been shown to be useful in testing programs and improving the software development process,

Parts of this research were supported by Contract F30602-85-C-0255 through Rome Air Development Center while the author was a graduate student at the Georgia Institute of Technology.

there has been no coherent way to integrate the various techniques. The Godzilla test data generator is an integrated collection of tools that supports the preparation, definition, modification, and creation of test data that is effective at detecting errors. Godzilla is a fully automated system that combines several technologies to support unit-level software testing during the development lifecycle.

The test data is based on the mutation analysis criterion and integrates such strategies as statement coverage, branch coverage, extremal testing, and symbolic evaluation. The test data is created from constraints that describe effective test cases. The technique that Godzilla implements is called constraint-based testing (CBT) [20]. CBT is a *fault-based* testing technique, which is a general strategy for testing software that tests for specific kinds of aults [6, 8, 18, 24]. Fault-based testing strategies succeed because programmers tend to make certain types of faults that can be well defined. This article focuses on the implementation of Godzilla. We begin by introducing unit-level software testing, the mutation criteria, and the Mothra and Godzilla systems. Next are the details of constraint-based testing. Section 3 gives the major algorithms and data structures of Godzilla's principle subsystems.

1.1. Software Testing

Although we have long been concerned with software correctness, software is now being applied in situations where it handles money (bank transactions, stock markets), safeguards human lives (airplanes, defense systems) and controls valuable machinery (factory robots, satellites). In critical situations such as these, software failures can be disastrous. Whenever we use software we risk some failure. The consequences of a failure can range from humorous to disastrous, but we would certainly like to find ways to reduce the amount of risk of using software.

The main purpose of software testing is to serve as a *risk-reducing* activity. Of course, we cannot eliminate all risk by determining that a program is correct [13], but we can reduce the risk of using software by finding and eliminating faults in the program. Reducing the risk of using a software program also increases our confidence that the software will perform as intended, which is another goal of software testing. Unit-level software testing is performed by choosing inputs, or *test cases*, for units and executing the software on the test cases to determine if the software is correct on those inputs.

Although testing can consume up to half of the cost of developing software [19], developing test cases is not only technically difficult, it is also tedious and repetitious. This is particularly true during unit testing, because of the level of detail with which the tester must be concerned. Thus, to test our software effectively, we need to find ways to automate unit testing.

In recent years, significant progress has been made toward automating the testing process. Improvements in technology have given us widely available software tools that automatically execute tests, report results, and help perform regression testing. These tools generally help the tester manage the testing process. One of the most difficult technical problems, however, is that of generating data with which to test the program units—and despite much active research, the bulk of this effort is still left to the tester. The Godzilla test data generator is an experimental prototype tool that automatically generates test data using mathematical constraints. Since constraint-based testing shares the same underlying theoretical basis as mutation analysis, mutation is introduced next.

1.2. Mutation Analysis

A set of test data is *adequate* for a program relative to a collection of faults if each fault will be detected by at least one test case. More formally,

Definition [8]. If P is a program to implement function F on domain D and Φ is a finite collection of programs, then a test set $T \subset D$ is adequate for P and F *relative* to Φ if $\forall$ programs $Q \in \Phi$, if $Q(D) \neq F(D) \Rightarrow \exists t \in T$ such that $Q(t) \neq F(t)$.

Relative adequate test sets are designed to cause specific variants of the program to fail, with the assumption that such test data will find most of the other faults. The faults considered by relative adequacy are commonly restricted by two principles, the *competent-programmer hypothesis* [2] and the *coupling effect* [8]. The competent-programmer hypothesis states that competent programmers tend to write programs that are "close" to being correct. In other words, a program written by a competent programmer may be incorrect, but it will differ from a correct version by only a few faults. The coupling effect states that a test data set that detects all simple faults in a program is so sensitive that it will also detect more complex faults. In other words, complex faults are coupled to simple faults. The coupling effect cannot be proved, but it has been demonstrated experimentally [21] and supported probabilistically [18]. The coupling effect allows us to focus on simple faults as test data that kills simple faults can also be expected to kill more complicated faults.

1.3. The Mothra Mutation System

During mutation analysis, faults are introduced into software by creating many versions of the software, each containing one fault (analogous to a hardware fault-injection experiment). Test data are used to execute these faulty programs with the goal of distinguishing the faulty program from the original. Hence the terminology; faulty programs are *mutants* of the original, and a mutant is *killed* by distinguishing the output of the mutant from that of the original program.

When a program is submitted to a mutation system, the system first creates mutant versions of the program. Next, test data are supplied to the system to serve as inputs to the program. Each test case is executed on the original program and the tester examines the output for correctness. If the output is incorrect, the test case has found a fault and the program must be corrected. If correct, the test case is executed on each live mutant. If the output of the mutant program is correct (as determined by a comparison with the original output), that mutant is marked dead and not executed against subsequent test cases. Some mutants are functionally equivalent to the original program and cannot be killed. After killing mutants, a *mutation score* is computed. If the total number of mutants is M, the number of dead mutants is D, and the number of equivalent mutants is E, the mutation score is the percentage of nonequivalent dead mutants:

$$MS(P, T) = \frac{D}{(M - E)}.$$

The mutation score is a close approximation of the relative adequacy of a test data set; a test set is relative adequate if its score is 100% (all mutants were killed). A benefit of the mutation score is that even if no errors are found, the mutation score still measures how well the software has been tested, giving the user information about the program in the absence of errors.

If (as is likely) mutants are still alive after mutant execution, the tester enhances the test data by supplying new inputs. The live mutants point out inadequacies in the test cases. In most cases, the tester creates test cases to kill individual live mutants. This process of adding new test cases, verifying correctness, and killing mutants is repeated until the tester is satisfied with the mutation score. A mutation score threshold can be set as a policy decision to require testers to test software to a predefined level. The effectiveness of this approach is based on a fundamental premise: if the software contains a fault, it is likely that there is a mutant that can only be killed by a test case that also reveals the fault. Mutation has been developed and experimented with for several years [1, 6, 11, 14, 16, 22, 25] and has been extensively applied to unit level testing. Although mutation has been largely automated [7], it has historically suffered from a lack of automated test-data generation. In previous mutation systems, testers had to generate test data manually, severely limiting the usefulness of the technique for large-scale efforts. Godzilla is a tool that automatically generates the test data for use in a mutation system, significantly extending the usefulness of mutation.

The most recent mutation system is Mothra [6], an integerated software testing environment that tests Fortran-77 programs. Programs are automatically translated by the front end of a compiler into an internal form consisting of a flexible symbol table and tuples of Mothra intermediate code (MIC) [15]. Test cases are stored and the program is executed by interpreting the internal form. The internal form is also used to generate mutations, which are stored as records that describe the changes to the MIC needed to create each mutant. Mothra interprets each live mutant against each available test case and reports the results.

1.4. The Godzilla Test Data Generation System

To generate mutation-adequate tests, a tester has traditionally interacted with interactive mutations system such as Mothra to examine remaining live mutants and design tests that kill them. Constraint-based testing automates this process by representing the conditions under which mutants die as mathematical constraints on program variables and automatically generating test cases that satisfy the constraints.

The Godzilla system contains the various program tools necessary to implement CBT. The system analyzes a test program, uses a rule-based system to model possible faults, creates constraints that describe test cases that will detect those faults, and finds values that satisfies those constraints to generate test cases for the test program. The Mothra/Godzilla tools were implemented in the programming language C on a DEC MicroVax II running the Berkeley Unix 4.3 operating system. The combined system contains about 50,000 lines of source code and has been successfully ported to a variety of machines, including a Vax 11/780, a Vas 8810, a Pyramid, and several Sun systems.

In the remainder of this article, the design and implementation of Godzilla's subsystems are described. Since Godzilla has been substantially evaluated and experiments have been reported elsewhere [6, 11, 20], this article focuses on how the system works rather than why. First, the concepts of CBT are discussed, then the software is described. The mechanisms we use to create and manipulate the constraints are described. Godzilla's architecture, important data structures, and algorithms are presented.

2. Constraint-based Testing

A software error has two components; a fault and a failure. A *fault* is an incorrect portion of the code. A *failure* is the external incorrect behavior exhibited by the software when a fault is triggered. If a program contains a fault, a given test case may or may not cause the fault to result in a failure. A test case that does cause a failure is said to trigger, or detect, the fault.

Godzilla develops test data to detect the same classes of faults that the Mothra software testing system uses. These faults are modeled by Mothra's *mutation operators* [15], which represent more than 10 years of refinement through several mutation systems. These operators explicitly require that the test data meet statement and branch coverage criteria, extremal values criteria, and domain perturbation. The mutation operators also directly model many types of faults. Thus, the test data that Godzilla generates will satisfy all these criteria—giving a set of test data that integrates several test data creation criteria.

Godzilla generates test data by posing the question: "What properties must the program inputs have to kill each mutant?" In brief, the inputs must cause the mutant program to have a program state that differs from the state of the original program after some execution of the mutated statement. Because faults are modeled as simple changes to single statements, an initial condition is that the mutated statement must be reached (the reachability condition). A further condition is that once the mutated statement is executed, the test case must cause the mutant program to behave erroneously—the fault that is being modeled must result in a failure in the program's behavior.

Godzilla describes these conditions on the test cases as mathematical systems of constraints. Reachability conditions are described by constraint systems called *path expressions*. Each statement in the program has a path expression that describes each execution path through the program to that statement. The condition that the test case must cause an erroneous state is described by a constraint that is specific to the type of fault being modeled by each mutation and requires that the computation performed by the mutated statement create an incorrect intermediate program state. This is called a *necessity constraint* because although an incorrect intermediate program state is necessary to kill the mutant, it is not sufficient to kill it. To kill the mutant, the test case must cause the program to create incorrect output, in which case the final state of the mutant program differs from that of the original program. Although satisfying the *sufficiency condition* is certainly desirable, it is impractical in practice. Completely determining the sufficiency condition implies knowing in advance the complete path a program will take, which is intractable. Godzilla conjoins each necessity constraint with the appropriate path expression constraint. The resulting constraint system is solved to generate a test case such that the constraint system is true.

2.1. Integrating Other Testing Techniques

By combining the reachability with the necessity condition, Godzilla integrates several well-known testing techniques into a single coherent test data generation scheme. Some of the testing techniques that Godzilla incorporates either directly or indirectly include statement coverage, branch coverage (and extended branch coverage), special values testing, domain perturbation, and symbolic evaluation.

Statement coverage [4] requires each statement in the program to be executed at least once. Godzilla incorporates this technique directly with the path expressions. Branch coverage [4] is a related technique that requires that every branch (both sides of each conditional) in the program be taken. This requirement is enforced by mutations of the program that can only be killed if each conditional evaluates to first be true, then false. In fact, the test data that Godzilla generates enforces the stronger requirement that every predicate in each conditional evaluate to be both true and false (extended branch coverage). For example, if a test program contains the conditional "IF $((A > B)$ AND $(X \geq Y))$," then branch coverage requires that the entire conditional evaluate to be true and false. Godzilla generates test data that forces $(A > B)$ to be both true and false, then $(X \geq Y)$ to be both true and false. Many failures occur because the program does not properly handle expressions that are negative, zero, or have some other special value [19]. Godzilla tests for these errors by generating test cases that cause each expression (and subexpression) to have the value zero, a negative, and a positive value.

Domain perturbation strategies partition the input space of a program into domains, where all test cases in each domain will cause the program to execute along the same path. Domain perturbation strategies attempt to select test data points that lie close to the boundaries of these domains. Mutation operators force test data to satisfy domain perturbation by modifying each expression in the program by a small amount (adding and subtracting 1 from integer expressions, 10% from real-valued expressions, etc.) and by substituting relational operators. Godzilla generates test data to satisfy the domain perturbation strategy by finding test data that will kill these mutants.

As explained in following sections, Godzilla uses symbolic evaluation as part of the procedure for generating the constraints. Godzilla also generates test data that are specific to mutation testing. For example, test cases are generated that force each variable to have values that are different from every other variable at that point in the program, which ensures the correct variable is being referenced. Part of the current work on this project is to find ways to integrate other testing techniques into the Godzilla system. It seems likely that many techniques for generating test data can be modeled as constraints on program variables. For example, path coverage strategies [3] require that specific statements, branches, or paths be executed. These strategies can be modeled by using constraints that are derived from the predicates that control the execution paths. Similarly, data flow methods [23] require that particular program subpaths be executed. These subpaths can be described using constraints derived from the predicates that control execution of the subpaths. These constraints can be incorporated into the Godzilla system to improve the power of the test data generated by Godzilla and to integrate the testing technique with constraint-based testing.

3. Implementation Godzilla

Godzilla's major functions are shown in Figure 1. These tools, designed as separate functions and implemented as separate programs, communicate through the files represented by ovals. The arrows in Figure 1 indicate the flow of information through the Godzilla system. The files are accessed through a common collection of routines that allow Godzilla's tools to view the files as abstract data types, promoting modularity and extensibility by giving each tool a uniform access to abstract routines that create, modify, store, and retrieve constraints. Integration of new testing techniques is therefore straightforward, as new tools can naturally use the same internal representation of constraints.

Adding the data flow capability discussed earlier, for example, would require only slight modification to the Godzilla system. A new subsystem for generating the data flow constraints would need to be added, but the already existing routines for creating, manipulating, and storing constraints could be used. Once generated, the data flow constraints could be reduced and satisfied using the same subsystems shown in Figure 1.

3.1. Representing Constraints

A constraint system in Godzilla is a hierarchical structure composed of expressions, constraints, and clauses arranged in disjunctive normal form. The basic component of a constraint system is an *algebraic expression*, which is composed of variables, parentheses, and programming language operators. Expressions are taken directly from the test program and come from right-hand sides of assignment statements, predicates within decision statements, etc.

A *constraint* is a pair of algebraic expressions related by one of the conditional operators $(>, <, =, \geq, \leq, \neq)$. Constraints evaluate to one of the binary values TRUE or FALSE and can be modified by the negation operator NOT $(\neg)$. A *clause* is a list of constraints connected by the two logical operators AND $(\wedge)$ and OR $(\vee)$. A *conjunctive clause* uses only the logical AND and a *disjunctive clause* uses only the logical OR. In the Godzilla system, all constraints are kept in *disjunctive normal form* (DNF), which is a series of conjunctive

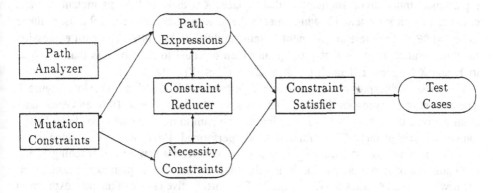

Figure 1. Godzilla automatic test case generator.

clauses connected by logical ORs. DNF is used for convenience during constraint generation and for ease of satisfaction (only one conjunctive clause needs to be satisfied).

Godzilla considers a *constraint system* to be a set of constraints that collectively represents one complete test case. A constraint system is often referred to as "constraints" or as a "constraint" when the distinction is obvious or unimportant. A constraint system is stored as a linked list of conjunctive clauses, each of which is a linked list of constraints. Each constraint, in turn, contains a relation and pointers to a left expression and a right expression.

In the following constraint system:

$$((X + Y \geq Z) \wedge (X \leq Y)) \vee (X > Z),$$

$X + Y$ is an expression and $(X + Y \geq Z)$ is a constraint. $((X + Y \geq Z) \wedge (X \leq Y))$ is a conjunctive clause, and the entire expression is a complete constraint system. Test cases such as $(X = 3, Y = 4, Z = 2)$, $(X = 3, Y = 4)$, and $(X = 4, Y = 1, Z = 3)$ satisfy the system.

3.2. Path Analyzer

The path analyzer uses the path coverage technique [3] to traverse the test program using the Mothra intermediate code (MIC) [15] to construct a path expression constraint for each statement. For each statement in the original program, the path analyzer creates a constraint such that if the test case reaches that statement, the constraint will be true. Note that we would ideally like to create constraints for the inverse; that if the constraint is satisfied, the statement will be executed. Creating constraints that guarantee reachability, however, implies a solution to the undecidable halting problem. In practical terms, however, the constraints we generate will guarantee execution of the targeted statement in the absence of back branches. In fact, the path expression constraints are strong enough to ensure that all statements are executed in the presence of back branches that have a structured form (i.e., loops).

For example, consider the subroutine MID shown in Figure 2 with one mutated statement. MID determines which of three integers is the median value. The mutation is a variable replacement mutation on statment 12 that replaces X with Y. To kill this mutant, the test case must reach statement 12, which means the tests in statements 2 and 9 must evaluate to be FALSE and the test in statement 11 must evaluate to be TRUE. The path expression for this mutation requires that Y be greater than or equal to Z, X be less than or equal to Y, and X be greater than Z, or $(Y \geq Z) \wedge (X \leq Y) \wedge (X > Z)$.

The partial path expression construction algorithm used in Godzilla is shown in Figure 3. The current path expression (CPE) is initially given the default value TRUE and each statement is given the value FALSE, indicating that no path to that statement has been found. On reaching a statement S, several actions are performed. First, the CPE is added to the previous path expression list for S (line 6). CPE represents a new way of reaching S, and each possible path to S is stored as a new disjunctive clause in the path expression. Next, the new PE for S becomes the CPE (line 7). Each disjunctive clause in the path expression

```
              INTEGER FUNCTION MID (X, Y, Z)
         C    MID is small and inefficient, but it
         C    does illustrate how Godzilla works.

              INTEGER X, Y, Z
     1        MID = Z
     2        IF (Y .LT. Z) THEN
     3           IF (X .LT. Y) THEN
     4              MID = Y
     5           ELSE IF (X .LT. Z) THEN
     6              MID = X
     7           ENDIF
     8        ELSE
     9           IF (X .GT. Y) THEN
    10              MID = Y
    11           ELSE IF (X .GT. Z) THEN
    12              MID = X
     Δ              MID = Y
    13           ENDIF
    14        ENDIF
              RETURN
```

Figure 2. MID.

Variables: *CPE* is the current path expression.

  PE [ ] contains the current path expression for each statement.

  P is the program.

  S and *S'* are statements in the program *P*.

  ρ is a predicate expression.

```
 1   CPE = TRUE
 2   for each statement S in P
 3      PE [S] = FALSE
 4   end
 5   for each statement S in P in order:
 6      PE [S] = PE [S] ∨ CPE
 7      CPE = PE [S]
 8      if S is a control flow statement then
            {ρ is the predicate of S, S' is the target of the branch.}
 9         Update CPE according the type of branch statement
10         PE [S'] = PE [S'] ∨ (PE [S] ∧ ρ)
11   end
```

Figure 3. Path expression algorithm.

flow statement, the CPE is updated by a modification rule that depends on S, and the conjunction of the CPE and the control flow predicate is added to the path expression of the branch's target statement (lines 9 and 10).

For example, suppose S is a GOTO statement. The CPE is added to the path expression list of the target statement for the GOTO. Next, the CPE is given the value of FALSE, because the statement following S cannot be reached through S—control always transfers. The modification rules for other control flow statements are similar and are based on predicate transformation rules for generating verification conditions (see, e.g., Chapter 3 of *Mathematical Theory of Computation* [17]). Note that the next statement to be examined during path analysis is not the target of the GOTO, but the next statement in the source code.

By disjuncting the current path expression to each statement's path expression (on line 6 in algorithm 3), each disjunct for a statement represents a distinct path to the statement. Because this algorithm makes one pass through the program, it does not propagate the predicates that control backbranches through the program. The algorithm does derive constraints that describe at least one path to each statement in the program, and the separate disjuncts represent all paths to a statement up to but not including loops. Obviously, directly including loops in this way would be impossible, since it would require an arbitrary number of disjuncts.

3.3. Mutation Constraint Generator

The constraint generator walks through the test program (again, using the MIC instructions) and for each statement applies rules that encode the mutations for that statement. For each mutant, the generator creates a constraint that describes the condition(s) on the variables that will cause the mutant program to compute an erroneous state.

Many mutations supported by Godzilla involve operand replacements. For these mutations, the constraint is that the original operand have a different value from the replacement operand. For example, the constraint is $(X \neq Y)$ for the mutant in Figure 2. When the mutation is involved in a predicate, just making the two operands unequal is unlikely to affect the (binary) predicate value. Thus, the necessity constraint is extended to force the value of the entire mutated predicate to be incorrect. For example, for the mutation that changes the reference to X on statement 11 to Y, instead of just $(X \neq Y)$, the constraint is $((X > Z) \neq (Y > Z))$.

Another class of mutations that Godzilla generates test cases for involve operator replacements. For a mutation of this type, the necessity constraints require the result of the entire mutated expression to differ from that of the original expression. Other mutations modify the entire statement; removing the statement or replacing the statement by a return. These mutations are included to model statement and path coverage strategies, so it is not surprising that there are no necessity constraints required to detect these mutations. The only requirement is that the test data cause the modified statement to be executed, which is enforced by the path expression constraint. The necessity constraints are described in complete detail elsewhere [10, 20].

3.4. Constraint Reducer

One difficulty that automated test data generation systems such as Godzilla have is concerned with handling internal variables. An *input* variable is part of the input set of a program—a value is included for the variable as part of the test case. A variable is *internal* to the program if it is not part of the input set. Internal variables are undefined when a program begins execution and are assigned values during execution (or not at all). Even though internal variables cannot be assigned values directly from the test case, they may still appear in constraints.

The internal variable problem is that of generating a test case to cause an internal variable to have a specific value at a particular point in the program's execution. The values of internal variables are computed within the program, but they are based on the program inputs. So even though the values of internal variables are not under a tester's direct control, they can be controlled indirectly. This problem is not new to constraint-based testing and is encountered in path testing strategies, among others. Although the problem is generally undecidable, internal variables can usually be symbolically described in terms of input variables using symbolic evaluation techniques [5, 23].

3.4.1. Symbolic Evaluation.

Symbolic evaluation of programs is related to actual execution much as symbolic algebra is related to arithmetic over numbers. Initially, input variables to the program are assigned symbolic values that are fixed, but unknown. For example, if a procedure has the parameters X and Y, then they may be given the symbolic values x and y. So if the value of a variable V is denoted by $v(V)$, then $v(X) = x$ and $v(Y) = y$.

Symbolic evaluation principally distinguishes between two types of statements: assignment statements and branching statements. During assignment statements, expressions are evaluated symbolically by extending the semantics of the operators in the expression. When symbolically executing the statement $A = 2 * X - Y$, we assign the symbolic value $(2 * x - y)$ to A. If the next statement is $B = Y + A$, then symbolic evaluation computes $v(B) = y + (2 * x - y) = 2 * x$.

When it reaches a conditional branching statement, the symbolic evaluator must take *both* branches. Consider an *if* statement of the form if E then S_1 else S_2, where E is a predicate expression and S_1 and S_2 are statements. During normal execution, either $v(E) = $ TRUE and S_1 is executed or $v(E) = $ FALSE and S_2 is executed. During symbolic evaluation however, $v(E)$ is a symbolic value and its boolean value is usually not known. Since both cases may be true, the symbolic evaluation splits into two executions, one of which assumes $v(E)$ and the other assumes $\neg v(E)$. Thus, over the course of the program, the symbolic evaluation forms a tree of executions where each node that has more than one outgoing arc represents a branch statement. In Godzilla, we represent this tree by forming disjunctive clauses.

3.4.2. Rewriting Constraints.

Godzilla (partially) solves the internal variable problem using symbolic evaluation. The routine used by Godzilla computes, for each variable, its symbolic value on each statement in the program. These symbolic values are lists of value-constraint pairs where the constraints represent the conditions under which the variable will have the symbolic value. These constraints are developed from the path expression disjuncts for the statement. For a variable X referenced at a statement S, X will have, at most, one value for each execution path that reaches S. Thus, each symbolic value for X has a path expression associated with it that describes the path to S that will cause X to have the value. These symbolic values are used to rewrite X in terms of input variables only.

As an example, consider the value of the return variable MID in Figure 2. At statement 1, MID is assigned the symbolic value Z. By assigning a value to Z, Godzilla can control the value of MID at the beginnings of statements 2–6 and 8–12. Because MID is assigned a new value at statements 4 and 6, its value at statement 7 depends on the execution path that was taken. The symbolic values for MID at statement 7 are:

$$MID = Y : (Y < Z) \wedge (X < Y),$$

$$MID = X : (Y < Z) \wedge (X \geq Y) \wedge (X < Z),$$

$$MID = Z : (Y < Z) \wedge (X \geq Y) \wedge (X \geq Z).$$

If MID appears in a constraint on statement 7, then the symbolic values X, Y, and Z can be substituted for MID, along with the associated path expression conditions. Similar symbolic values for MID are computed for statements 13 and 14. Note that MID is undefined at statement 1. When an undefined variable appears in a constraint, that variable is considered to have a constant value. This is not particularly important for test case generation because faults involving undefined variables tend to be easy to detect by even the most obvious test cases.

3.4.3. Computing Internal Variable Expressions.

Solving for internal variables is a two-step process. First, we use symbolic evaluation to construct a table of symbolic values for the internal variables. Then these values are used to rewrite the internal variables in terms of constants and input variables. When an internal variable needs a value to solve a constraint, a value is chosen and the associated constraints are added to the constraint system being solved.

The algorithm to compute symbolic values for internal variables is shown in Figure 4. After execution, each ⟨value:constraint⟩ pair in *IVExpr* represents the conditions necessary for the internal variable to take on that value at the statement.

After the expressions have been calculated, they are used to resolve internal variables in the constraint systems. The algorithm to resolve internal variables is shown in Figure 5. When a value is needed for an internal variable, the IVExpr table furnishes an appropriate ⟨value:constraint⟩ pair. The value is used to resolve the internal variable (line 4) and the associated constraint is added to the system of constraints being rewritten (line 6).

After execution, the internal variable *iv* has been eliminated from the system of constraints C. Note that there may be several ⟨value:constraint⟩ pairs in the IVExpr table that could be used. Obviously the value chosen for *iv* must satisfy the constraints. Beyond that, it does not matter and Godzilla uses the heuristic of choosing the value with the simplest associated constraint.

3.4.4. Other Constraint Reductions.

When rewriting constraints in terms of input variables, the symbolic evaluator often introduces redundant or contradictory constraints. Godzilla's constraint reducer attempts to recognize and reduce as many of these constraints as possible.

Variables: *CPred* is the current predicate.

Pred [ ] contains the current predicate for each statement.

IVExpr [ ] [ ] contains the expressions for each internal variable. For each statement and internal variable, it contains a list of ⟨value:constraint⟩ pairs.

s is a statement in the program *P*.

iv is an internal variable in the program *P*.

```
1    CPred = TRUE
2    for each statement s in P
3      Pred [s] = FALSE
4      for each internal variable iv:
5        IVExpr [s] [iv] = nil
6      end
7    end
8    for each statement s in P in order
9      Pred [s] = Pred [s] ∨ CPred
10     CPred = Pred [s]
11   if s is an assignment statement then
12     [Use s to form lhs = rhs]
       Add ⟨rhs : CPred⟩ to IVExpr [s] [lhs]
13   if s is a control flow statement then
14     Update CPred according the type of branch statement
15   end
```

Figure 4. Internal variable expression algorithm.

Variables: *C* is the current disjunctive normal form constraint system.

IVExpr [ ] [ ] is the table of internal variable expressions.

iv is the internal variable to be resolved.

value is the value that is returned for *iv*.

c is the constraint that is necessary for *iv* = *value*.

s is the statement that the current constraint refers to.

cl is a clause in *C*.

```
1    Retrieve a ⟨value:constraint⟩ pair from IVExpr [s] [iv] into value and c.
2    for each clause cl in C:
3      if cl contains iv then
4        Substitute value for iv
5    end
6    Append c to C (C = C ∧ c)
```

Figure 5. Internal variable resolution algorithm.

Assume that X and Y are input variables and A and B are internal variables. Consider the statement

$$X = A + B$$

and the following symbolic values for A and B:

$$A = \begin{cases} 3 & \text{if } Y < 0 \\ 5 & \text{if } Y \geq 0 \end{cases} \qquad B = \begin{cases} 9 & \text{if } Y < 7 \\ 12 & \text{if } Y \geq 7 \end{cases}$$

To compute the possible symbolic values for X, we substitute these expressions into the assignment:

$$X = \begin{cases} 3 + 9 & \text{if } (Y < 0) \wedge (Y < 7) \\ 3 + 12 & \text{if } (Y < 0) \wedge (Y \geq 7) \\ 5 + 9 & \text{if } (Y \geq 0) \wedge (Y < 7) \\ 5 + 12 & \text{if } (Y \geq 0) \wedge (Y \geq 7) \end{cases}$$

Although this symbolic representation of the values for X is complete and correct, the clauses contain two redundant constraints and one contradictory constraint that can be eliminated. Also, the constant expressions for X can be evaluated to constant values. The first value, $3 + 9$, will be assigned to X if $((Y < 0) \wedge (Y < 7))$ is true. Because $(Y < 0)$ subsumes $(Y < 7)$, the second constraint is eliminated. Similarly, in the last value, $5 + 12$, the clause $((Y \geq 0) \wedge (Y \geq 7))$ is reduced to $(Y \geq 7)$. The second value $3 + 12$ is assigned to X if $((Y < 0) \wedge (Y \geq 7))$ is true. Because this is a contradiction, this entire symbolic value is eliminated. The reduced symbolic value for X is

$$X = \begin{cases} 12 & \text{if } Y < 0 \\ 14 & \text{if } (Y \geq 0) \wedge (Y < 7) \\ 17 & \text{if } (Y \geq 7) \end{cases}$$

These types of reductions are performed on the complete constraint system *after* internal variables have been rewritten to be input variables. Godzilla does not completely reduce the constraints; it only applies reductions that will eliminate much of the redundancy we have observed. Much of the redundancy is inherent in the path expressions. The contradictory clauses often represent infeasible paths in the program or necessity constraints that cannot be true if a particular path is taken. Eliminating redundant and contradictory constraints is particularly important to the efficient execution of the constraint satisfier, largely because rewriting the internal variables results in larger and more complicated constraint systems.

3.5. Constraint Satisfier

The last step in generating test cases is to find values that satisfy the constraint systems. Finding values to satisfy a constraint system is a difficult problem that arises in such diverse areas as computability theory, operations research, and artificial intelligence. The Godzilla system employs heuristics that work efficiently and produce satisfying test cases quickly when the constraints have a simple form, and more slowly when the constraints are more complicated.

Initially, each variable is assigned a domain of possible values that a variable can have. Theoretically, this *values domain* includes all values that a variable of that type can have on the machine being used. In practice, the values domain can be reduced by the user and by default, Godzilla assigns numeric variables the values domain of -100 to 100. Each constraint in a constraint system is considered to reduce the values domain for the variable(s) in the constraint. Constraints of the form $(X \, \Re \, k)$, where X is a variable, k is a constant, and $\Re$ is a relational operator, are used to reduce the current values domain for X. For example, if X is an integer and has the constraint $(X > 0)$, the values domain becomes 1 to 100. Constraints of the form $(X \, \Re \, Y)$, where both X and Y are variables, are used to reduce the values domain of both X and Y. When the values domain for a variable is reduced to one value, that value becomes the test case value for that variable. This value is then substituted into all remaining constraints that contain the variable. If the values domain for a variable is reduced to zero values, the constraint system has become infeasible.

The domain reduction procedure is shown in Figure 6. It uses an array of domains, one for each input variable. The procedure uses the constraints to successively reduce the size of each variable's domain until a value is assigned. For each variable, a constant ϵ is assumed to exist that is the smallest separation between two values of that type. The procedure in Figure 6 uses the subroutine ADJ_OPER in Figure 7.

When no additional simplification can be done, a value is chosen for one of the remaining variables (line 28 through line 34 in Figure 6). Godzilla uses the heuristic of using the variable with the smallest values domain, hoping the value will have less chance of causing a solvable constraint system to become unsolvable. The value is chosen arbitrarily from the values domain and is back substituted into the remaining constraints. Then the modified constraints are used to modify the values domain as described above. This process is repeated until all input variables have been assigned a value.

Each time a variable is assigned a value, the satisfying space for the constraint system is reduced by one dimension, progressively simplifying the constraints in the constraint system. If chosen poorly, the new value may make the region infeasible. An underlying assumption is that because of the simple form of the test case constraints, the new values seldom make the constraint system infeasible. When they do, the infeasiblity is often recognized since they show up as conflicting constraints such as $(X = 4 \wedge X > 8)$, or a values domain of some variable becomes empty.

When a constraint system becomes infeasible after one or more value assignments, the procedure is repeated with the original constraint system. Experimentation [11] has found that the domain reduction procedure finds solutions to feasible constraint systems in an average of 4 iterations (with an upper bound of about 25). Although this seems wasteful, this can be put in perspective by noting that 25 executions of the satisfaction procedure requires less machine time than one execution of the resultant test case on the test program— and each test case is ultimately executed dozens or hundreds of times. We are currently exploring ways of improving the satisfaction procedure by employing more efficient search procedures, but these have not, as yet, been implemented.

Variables: TC [ ] is an array of values, indexed by the variables in the constraints.
C is the system of constraints.
x and y are variables.
D [ ] is an array of *domains*, one for each variable. D [x] contains the
list of (current) upper and lower bounds on x, D [x] $= (a_x : b_x)$.
R is a set of newly resolved variables.
c is a constraint.
v is a value.
k is a constant.
γ is one of the conditional operations $\{>, <, =, \geq, \leq, \neq\}$.

```
1    TC [x] = undefined, for each x in C
2    R = { }
3    loop
4      repeat
5        for each x in R
6          replace each x in C with the value TC [x]
7        end for
8        for each c in C of the form x γ k
9          ADJUST_OPER (D [x], γ, k)     (* defined in Figure 7. *)
10         if aₓ > bₓ then return INFEASIBLE
11         if aₓ = bₓ then
12           TC [x] = k
13           R = R ∪ {x}
14           remove c from C
15         end for
16       until R = { }
17       for each c in C of the form x γ y
18         choose an arbitrary value v for x from D [x] such that (aₓ ≤ v ≤ bₓ):
19         TC [x] = v
20         c = v γ y
21         ADJUST_OPER (D [y], γ, v)     (* defined in Figure 7. *)
22         if aᵧ > bᵧ then return INFEASIBLE
23         if aᵧ = bᵧ then
24           TC [y] = aᵧ
25           R = R ∪ {y}
26           remove c from C
27       end for
28       if R = { } then
29         if ∃x where TC [x] = undefined then
30           choose an arbitrary value v for x from D [x] such that (aₓ ≤ v ≤ bₓ):
31           TC [x] = v
32           R = R ∪ {x}
33         else
34           return FEASIBLE
35    end loop
```

Figure 6. Domain reduction procedure.

```
    Subroutine ADJUST_OPER (Domain, γ, k)
    Variables:  Domain is the upper and lower bound, Domain = (aₓ : bₓ).
                γ is a conditional operator {>, <, =, ≥, ≤, ≠}.
                k is a constant.
1       adjust Domain according to the operator γ:
2          if γ is "≥" then
3             Domain = (k : bₓ)
4          if γ is "≤" then
5             Domain = (aₓ : k)
6          if γ is "≠" then
7             Domain = (aₓ : k − ε, k + ε : bₓ)
8          if γ is "<" then
9             Domain = (aₓ : k − ε)
10         if γ is ">" then
11            Domain = (k + ε : bₓ)
12         if γ is "=" then
13            Domain = (k : k)
14      end ADJUST_OPER
```

Figure 7. Adjust operator subroutine.

The initial values domains for the variables can increase the procedure's efficiency by reducing the size of the search space. For example, if it is known that the program being tested does not need to accept negative values, the initial values domains may start at zero. Or, if the first step in the test program is to test for negative inputs, we may wish to use some negative numbers as inputs, but the majority of the test cases will require positive numbers. In this case, the technique will find a solution more quickly if the initial domain is adjusted to include only a few negative values. Because the domain needs to be at least large enough to contain all the constraints, limiting the domain is difficult to do automatically and is usually done manually by someone who is familiar with the test program.

Although domain reduction always terminates, it does not always generate a correct solution. It does, however, succeed for a large percentage of the test case constraints that are derived from actual software. In our experiments, we have yet to encounter a feasible constraint system that was not satisfied by Godzilla [11]. The randomness that is part of the procedure is important because we often satisfy constraint systems multiple times to generate different test cases for the same mutation.

4. Conclusions

The Godzilla system is a fully automated test data generator for a fault-based testing strategy. It not only demonstrates that software test data generation for mutation can be automated at a level beyond that of previous research or commercially available systems, but it also provides a vehicle for integrating many current testing techniques. The fact that Godzilla is based on constraints, and that the software is built in a modular fashion, makes it quick and easy to integrate still more error-detection capabilities into the system.

Godzilla is very much a "plug-compatible" system. Adding new modules that generate different constraints is straightforward, as there are routines in the constraint handling module for treating constraints as an abstract data type. For example, user-defined constraints in the form of assertions that are placed into the source program have recently been added. Assertions were integrated into Godzilla by adding one subsystem to translate the assertions into constraints that are created and stored using the preexisting constraint handling routines described in Section 3.1. These assertion constraints are handled uniformly by both the constraint reducer described in Section 3.4 and the constraint satisfier described in Section 3.5. This modularity allows the constraint satisfier in Godzilla to incorporate new types of constraints in an all but invisible manner. We are currently considering ways to incorporate data flow testing [4, 23] into Godzilla.

The theoretical limitations of the techniques used by Godzilla are daunting. Generating path expressions that guarantee reachability is generally undecidable, guaranteeing that test cases that satisfy the necessity constraints will kill the mutant is undecidable, and the satisfaction procedure will sometimes fail. On the other hand, as a practical engineering tool, Godzilla invariably succeeds in generating effective test cases for unit testing. This is not because magic solutions have been found to undecidable problems but because partial solutions work very well in practical situations. It only takes one instance of a problem to make the general problem very difficult—but if the vast majority of the times the problem can be solved quickly and efficiently then we as practitioners have found a useful solution.

Acknowledgments

It would like to thank Jason Seaman of Clemson University for implementing much of the constraint rewriting software and for supplying the example in Section 3.4.4.

References

1. A.T. Acree, "On mutation," Ph.D. dissertation, Georgia Institute of Technology, Atlanta, GA, 1980.
2. A.T. Acree, T.A. Budd, R.A. DeMillo, R.J. Lipton, and F.G. Sayward, "Mutation analysis," Technical Report GIT-ICS-79/08, School of Information and Computer Science, Georgia Institute of Technology, Atlanta, GA, September 1979.
3. L.A. Clarke, "A system to generate test data and symbolically execute programs," *IEEE Trans. Software Eng.* vol. 2, no. 3, pp. 215–222, September 1976.
4. L.A. Clarke, A. Podgurski, D.J. Richardson, and S.J. Zeil, "A comparison of data flow path selection criteria," in *Proc. Eighth Int. Conf. Software Eng.*, London UK, pp. 244–251, August 1985.
5. L.A. Clarke and D.J. Richardson, "Applications of symbolic evaluation," *J. Syst. Software*, vol. 5, no. 1, pp. 15–35, 1985.
6. R.A. DeMillo, D.S. Guindi, K.N. King, W.M. McCracken, and A.J. Offutt, "An extended overview of the Mothra software testing environment," in *Proc. Second Workshop Software Testing, Verification, and Analysis*, Banff, Alberta, Canada, pp. 142–151, July 1988.
7. R.A. DeMillo, E.W. Krauser, R.J. Martin, A.J. Offutt, and E.H. Spafford, "The Mothra tool set," in *Proc. 22nd Hawaii Int. Conf. Syst. Sci.*, Kailua-Kona, HI, pp. 275–284, January 1989.
8. R.A. DeMillo, R.J. Lipton, and F.G. Sayward, "Hints on test data selection: Help for the practicing programmer," *IEEE Computer* vol. 11, no. 4, pp. 34–41, April 1978.
9. R.A. DeMillo, W.M. McCracken, R.J. Martin, and J.F. Passafiume, *Software Testing and Evaluation*. Benjamin/Cummings: Menlo Park, CA, 1987.

10. R.A. DeMillo and A.J. Offutt, "Constraint-based automatic test data generation," *IEEE Trans. Software Eng.* vol. 17, no. 9, September 1991.

11. R.A. DeMillo and A.J. Offutt, "Experimental results of automatically generated adequate test sets," in *Proc. Sixth Annual Pacific Northwest Software Quality Conf.*, Portland, OR, pp. 209–232, September 1988.

12. J.B. Goodenough, "A survey of program issues," in P. Wegner, ed., *Research Directions in Software Technology.* Prentice-Hall: Englewood Cliffs, NJ, 1979, pp. 316–340.

13. W.E. Howden, "Reliability of the path analysis testing strategy," *IEEE Trans. Software Eng.* vol. 2, no. 3, pp. 208–215, September 1976.

14. W.E. Howden, "Weak mutation testing and completeness of test sets," *IEEE Trans. Software Eng.* vol. 8, no. 4, pp. 371–379, July 1982.

15. K.N. King and A.J. Offutt, "A Fortran language system for mutation-based software testing," *Software Practice and Experience* vol. 21, no. 7, pp. 686–718, July 1991.

16. R.J. Lipton and F.G. Sayward, "The status of research on program mutation," in *Digest for the Workshop on Software Testing and Test Documentation*, pp. 355–373, December 1978.

17. Z. Manna, *Mathematical Theory of Computation.* McGraw-Hill: New York, 1974.

18. L.J. Morell, "Theoretical insights into fault-based testing," in *Proc. Second Workshop on Software Testing, Verification, and Analysis*, Banff, Alberta, Canada, pp. 45–62, July 1988.

19. G. Myers, *The Art of Software Testing.* Wiley: New York, 1979.

20. A.J. Offutt, "Automatic test data generation," Ph.D. dissertation, Georgia Institute of Technology, Atlanta, GA, 1988. Technical Report GIT-ICS 88/28 (also released as Purdue University Software Engineering Research Center Technical Report SERC-TR-25-P).

21. A.J. Offutt, "The coupling effect: Fact or fiction?" in *Proc. Third Symp. on Software Testing, Analysis, and Verification*, Key West, FL, pp. 131–140, December 1989.

22. A.J. Offutt, "Using mutation analysis to test software," in *Proc. Seventh International Conference on Testing Computer Software*, San Francisco, CA, pp. 65–77, June 1990.

23. S. Rapps and W.J. Weyuker, "Selecting software test data using data flow information," *IEEE Trans. Software Eng.* vol. 11, no. 4, pp. 367–375, April 1985.

24. E.J. Weyuker, "Assessing test data adequacy through program inference," *ACM Trans. Programming Languages Syst.* vol. 5, no. 4, pp. 641–655, October 1983.

25. M.R. Woodward and K. Halewood, "From weak to strong, dead or alive? An analysis of some mutation testing issues," in *Proc. Second Workshop on Software Testing, Verification, and Analysis*, Banff, Alberta, Canada, pp. 152–158, July 1988.